Developmental Disabilities

Some of the chapters in this book were prepared pursuant to a grant from the Developmental Disabilities Office, Office of Human Development Services, U.S. Department of Health, Education and Welfare. Grantees undertaking such projects under government sponsorship are encouraged to express freely their judgment in professional and technical matters. Points of view or opinions do not, therefore, necessarily represent official BDD, OHDS, DHEW position or policy.

Developmental Disabilities

The DD Movement

Edited by

Ronald Wiegerink, Ph.D.
Director, Developmental Disabilities Technical Assistance System,
Frank Porter Graham Child Development Center, Chapel Hill;
Professor, Division of Special Education,
University of North Carolina at Chapel Hill

and

John W. Pelosi, Ph.D.
Associate Director for Planning and Evaluation,
Developmental Disabilities Technical Assistance System;
Associate Professor, Division of Special Education,
University of North Carolina at Chapel Hill

·P A U L·H·
BROOKES
PUBLISHERS

Baltimore

Paul H. Brookes, Publishers
Post Office Box 10624
Baltimore, Maryland 21204

362.30973
Dev

Typeset by The Composing Room of Michigan, Inc. (Grand Rapids)
Manufactured in the United States of America by The Maple Press Company
(York, Pennsylvania)

Library of Congress Cataloging in Publication Data
Main entry under title:

Developmental disabilities.

  Includes index.
  1. Developmentally disabled—United States.
2. Developmentally disabled services—United States.
3. Developmentally disabled—Legal status, laws, etc.—
United States. I. Wiegerink, Ronald, 1939-
II. Pelosi, John W.
HV3006.A4D48   362.3'0973   79-15516
ISBN 0-933716-02-8

Contents

Contributors

Paula (Hammer) Breen, M.S. (Public Health); Professional Fellow with the Bush Institute for Child and Family Policy, Frank Porter Graham Child Development Center, Chapel Hill, North Carolina

Iris Buhl, M.A. (Special Education); member of Regional Intervention Program Evaluation Committee, Nashville, Tennessee

Sondra Diamond, M.Ed. (Counseling and Guidance); private practice, Philadelphia, Pennsylvania

Charles R. Horejsi, D.S.W.; Professor of Social Work, University of Montana, Missoula

Toby Knox, B.A.; President of Creative Communications Associates, Inc., Montpelier, Vermont

Donald O. Mayer, J.D.; Attorney in private practice, Asheville, North Carolina

G. Ronald Neufeld, Ph.D.; Executive Director of British Columbia Association of Mental Retardation and Executive Director of British Columbia Mental Retardation Institute, Delta, British Columbia

Vince Parrish, M.A. (Special Education); Principal of Regional Intervention Program, Nashville, Tennessee

Gary Richman, M.A. (Communication); President of a consulting firm specializing in training and materials related to human services for handicapped persons, Chapel Hill, North Carolina

Donald J. Stedman, Ph.D.; Associate Vice President for Academic Affairs, University of North Carolina

Pascal L. Trohanis, Ph.D.; Associate Professor of Education, University of North Carolina at Chapel Hill

Ann P. Turnbull, Ph.D.; Associate Professor, Division of Special Education, University of North Carolina at Chapel Hill

H. Rutherford Turnbull, III, J.D., Master of Laws; Professor of Public Law and Government, Institute of Government, University of North Carolina at Chapel Hill

Rita Varela, M.A. (Political Science); Special Projects Manager for American Coalition of Citizens with Disabilities, Washington, D.C.

Frank Warren, Director of the information referral service of the National Society for Autistic Children, Washington, D.C.

Ronald Wiegerink, Ph.D.; Professor, Division of Special Education, University of North Carolina at Chapel Hill; Director of Developmental Disabilities Technical Assistance System, Frank Porter Graham Child Development Center, Chapel Hill

Laurence Wiseman, Vice President of the marketing research firm of Yankelovich, Skelly and White, Inc., New York

Preface

Since 1972, the Developmental Disabilities Technical Assistance System has produced straightforward, nontechnical exposition of topics of major concern to handicapped persons and their advocates. Each of these was designed to shed light on the evolution of the developmental disabilities movement in this country. These writings covered a wide variety of topics, but all were written to be readily understandable to professionals and consumers alike and to make knowledge available and usable. Many of these writings have received acclaim for this very reason; acclaim has come from users and in annual awards from the Society for Technical Communication.

Part I of the book describes the backdrop of the developmental disabilities movement: the nature and needs of persons with developmental disabilities, the role and function of the states' Developmental Disabilities Planning Councils, and a critique of the movement to date. Part II presents the advocacy mission of the movement, the very heart and soul of the program. Several different types of advocacy are examined: systems advocacy, legal advocacy, and personal advocacy. Part III presents chapters which describe the public awareness thrust of the movement. Public awareness has been perhaps the movement's most often used method to bring about change and its most important product to date. Public awareness of the needs and rights of persons with developmental disabilities has increased a hundred fold in the last eight years. Part IV describes some of the services and service issues that make up the uncoordinated network of services now in place. Finally, the last chapter provides a review and perspective on the future of human services. In total, these writings describe a movement that has grown and flourished in spite of monumental barriers that exist in the political and organizational make-up of human services today.

In this volume we have tried to capture the essence and variety of Developmental Disabilities Technical Assistance System publications. We have included these articles because they communicate effectively, continue to be relevant, and make conceptual contributions to the field of developmental disabilities. Drawn from a variety of vantage points represented by respected authorities, the contributions are written by educators, attorneys, service administrators, counselors, consumers, and observers. We have labored to put together a resource book that will provide the individual interested in the developmental disabilities movement with a relevant and broad perspective on the program.

Ronald Wiegerink
John W. Pelosi

Developmental Disabilities

Part I
DEVELOPMENTAL DISABILITIES

Part I includes five chapters about the developmental disabilities (DD) movement. Collectively these provide a description of the movement, its origin, its focus, and its raison d'être. They also articulate important points of emphasis inherent to the DD concept. Certain problems, constraints, and controversial aspects are analyzed and discussed, providing important insight into the dynamics associated with the development of the DD movement.

The first chapter by Paula Breen and Gary Richman, "The Evolution of the Developmental Disabilities Concept," is an updated excerpt from *The Orientation Notebook* written by them. It presents the thinking upon which the concept of DD is based. This chapter describes the evolution of this concept in terms of legislative and definitional changes. It also includes discussion about certain controversial aspects of the DD concept. These are reflected not only in the definition, but in the philosophical orientation of those concerned with the implementation of the DD program as well.

The next chapter, "Profile of Developmental Disabilities," includes information about four of the primary types of handicapping conditions included under the rubric of developmental disabilities: mental retardation, cerebral palsy, autism, and epilepsy. It also emphasizes an important point in the DD concept, that although there may be differences in diagnostic labels, there are substantial commonalities in services needed. This chapter is an edited version of the narrative portion of a slide-tape presentation produced by National Foundation of Dentistry for the Handicapped and DDTAS. It presents the etiology and characteristics associated with each type of disability. It also provides information about the number of people who have each disability. Information about service needs and service provision is also included.

One component of the DD movement that has been instrumental in its development is the state-level Developmental Disabilities Council. To be knowledgeable about the DD movement in any particular state, one must become informed about the performance of its DD Council. To know what to look for, Sondra Diamond's "Developmentally Disabled Persons: Their Rights and Needs for Services" should be helpful. It begins with her Bill of Rights for the

Disabled, which provides an excellent context for Ms. Diamond's poignant account of her own experiences as a person with a handicapping condition. She weaves her experiences with those of others to produce a fabric that is graphic in its portrayal of how society at large behaves toward those who are different from its norm. Ms. Diamond's article provides thoughtful examination of flaws and contradictions in our legal structure and our service structure that seriously constrain efforts to maximize the potential of handicapped people. She further challenges all of us to look within ourselves and to reexamine our own reactions to people who have handicapping conditions.

"The DD Council and Its Membership" is another updated excerpt from *The Orientation Notebook* by Paula Breen and Gary Richman. It describes the congressional intent of the role and function of the DD Council and how the Council's role and function have been altered and strengthened through legislative changes as well as some of the thinking behind these changes. DD Council membership is discussed along with an analysis of changes in composition of the Council brought about by recent legislative action. The chapter also includes observations about DD Council staffing patterns, how these vary from state to state, and how Congress has responded to Councils' need to have sufficient staff.

The final chapter in this part is entitled "Two Faces of the National Developmental Disabilities Movement." In it, Ronald Wiegerink contrasts two opposing perspectives on the DD movement; the optimists and the cynics. After characterizing the position of these different views, his article delineates a number of the problems that have constrained development of the DD movement. He includes philosophical, organizational, political, and economic problems. Dr. Wiegerink points out the progress made and the positive results obtained by actions within the DD movement, both on a national and state basis. He concludes his chapter with an optimistic statement about the direction of the DD movement.

1
Evolution of the Developmental Disabilities Concept

Paula Breen and Gary Richman

The first federal developmental disabilities law, PL 91-517, Developmental Disabilities Services and Facilities Construction Act, enacted in 1970, set forth this legal definition of developmental disability:

> The term "developmental disability" means a disability attributable to mental retardation, cerebral palsy, epilepsy, or another neurological condition of an individual found by the Secretary to be closely related to mental retardation or to require treatment similar to that required for mentally retarded individuals, which disability originates before such individual attains age eighteen, which has continued or can be expected to continue indefinitely, and which constitutes a substantial handicap to such individuals.

The definition clusters three categorical disorders: mental retardation, cerebral palsy, and epilepsy. It is important to understand the thinking of those who developed the definition. In 1970 empirical data were available on two points: 1) all three of the conditions are major causes of substantial handicap to adults disabled in childhood and 2) all three of the disorders imply multiple handicaps requiring special and similar services throughout childhood and adult life. Let us review the data.

1. In 1970 Social Security figures showed mental retardation, cerebral palsy, and epilepsy to be the leading causes of disability in adults whose handicap originated in childhood. These three disorders accounted for 80% of all adults disabled in childhood receiving Social Security benefits. Thus of all handicapping conditions that affect children, mental retardation, cerebral palsy, and epilepsy command attention as long-term, chronic, and severe impairments.
2. There is ample evidence of multiple handicaps and of the overlapping of the three conditions clinically. Of the 750,000 individuals with cerebral

palsy, two-thirds are also mentally retarded. An estimated 20% to 30% of epileptic individuals are mentally retarded (Conley, 1973). Of institutionalized mentally retarded persons, one-half have seizure disorders.

The facts further show that a primary diagnosis of any one of the three—mental retardation, cerebral palsy, or epilepsy—is likely to be accompanied by a wide spectrum of other disabilities. Of all individuals with cerebral palsy, 70% have speech and communication disorders, one-third have visual problems, and one-fifth have learning disabilities. Slightly over 30% of retarded children suffer additional physical handicaps and perhaps 40% suffer psychiatric problems (Conley, 1973). Thus there were empirical indicators of some commonality among the three disorders.

The concept of developmental disability recognizes that the commonality of service needs among people with long-term, substantial (often multiple) handicaps did not fit into the categorical programs enacted during the 1960's. Somehow the categorical programs were designed for people with moderate disabilities and not tailored to the individual needs of the severely disabled. The multiply handicapped and the severely handicapped just did not get served. There was a growing awareness of the inadequacies of using diagnostic tags to deliver services.

At about the same time advocates for the handicapped were becoming increasingly sensitive to the inherent dangers of "labeling." For a complete discussion of the labeling phenomena, consult *The Futures of Children: Categories, Labels, and Their Consequences* (Hobbs, 1974).

The data, the disenchantment with categories, and the new sensitivity to labeling converged in a call for a functional definition of *handicap*. The original DD legislation was, in a sense, paradoxical, combining a functional definition and three categorical groups. However, its underlying philosophy and its clear intent was a functional, noncategorical approach to severe disability originating in childhood (before age 18). Hobbs states that "conceptually the Developmental Disabilities Legislation is quite advanced in identifying a special group on the basis of service needs rather than symptoms or status."

The 1975 legislation maintained the paradox. The primary thrust of the developmental disabilities concept continued to be a functional, noncategorical approach. Yet the law added a fourth category, autism, for the same reasons that the original three were grouped together. The question of adding a fifth category was one of the major controversies in the congressional debate over the new Developmental Disability Act. The issue was whether to exclude all learning disabilities, to include them all, to include only "severe specific learning disabilities" (as in the Senate version), or to include dyslexia only (as in the House version). The result was a compromise. In the Act's definition of developmental disabilities, dyslexia is specifically mentioned, but it is effectively excluded as a separate disorder. According to the 1975 federal legislation, a dyslexic individual may be included only if his condition is attributable to mental retardation, epilepsy, cerebral palsy, autism, or a closely related condition. The compromise recognized the seriousness of dyslexia, but it reflected Congress's view that it is primarily an educational problem, whereas a developmental disability requires consideration of a broad range of service needs.

In the wake of the debate over the 1975 legislation, a considerable effort was launched to study the appropriateness of the definition of developmental disabilities. As a result, the Developmentally Disabled Assistance and Bill of Rights Act (PL 95-602), signed by President Carter in November, 1978, has succeeded in more closely capturing the noncategorical spirit upon which the DD movement was founded. Rather than continuing to expand the list of handicapping conditions, the 1978 legislation defines a developmental disability functionally. The new act states that the term *developmental disability* is a severe, chronic disability attributed to a mental and/or physical impairment, which is manifested before the person reaches age 22. It is likely to continue indefinitely and results in substantial functional limitations in three or more of the following areas of major life activity: self-care, learning, self-direction, economic sufficiency, receptive and expressive language, mobility, or capacity for independent living. Finally, it reflects the person's need for a combination and sequence of special, interdisciplinary, or generic care, treatment, or other services that are of lifelong or extended duration and are individually planned and coordinated.

A special report to Congress is required by January, 1981, on the impact of the definition, including an analysis of the impact on each of the categories of persons served before the passage of this legislation as to the numbers served; amounts expended; and an assessment, evaluation, and comparison of services. In addition, the Joint Senate-House Conference Report (1978), which accompanied the legislation, states that the new definition is intended to cover everybody currently covered and that those with specified conditions—autism, cerebral palsy, dyslexia, epilepsy, or mental retardation—are included if they meet the functional criteria. The report also states that services provided to these individuals should not be diminished, and, furthermore, that a reasonable proportion of any new funding is expected to be directed to individuals with these disabilities.

In spite of the functional definition of a developmental disability the paradox concerning the exact nature of the DD program lingers on. The functional definition implies a broad-based planning and advocacy approach aimed at all persons with long-term severe disabilities which are manifested before 22 years of age. However, the Conference Report, coupled with the new legislative provisions regarding the use of DD funds, implies that the DD program is, at least in large part, a service provision program with preferences for specified categorical groups.

REFERENCES

Conference Report. Comprehensive rehabilitation services amendments of 1978. (PL 95-602) US House of Representatives Report No. 95-1780. To accompany HR 12467. 95th Congress Second Session. October 13, 1978.

Conley, R. *Economics of Mental Retardation*. Baltimore: Johns Hopkins Press, 1973.

Hobbs, N. *The Futures of Children: Categories, Labels and Their Consequences*. Nashville, Vanderbilt University, 1974.

2
Profile of Developmental Disabilities

Developmental disabilities is a recent term, born in federal legislation in 1970 to signal a new concept and philosophy of services for persons handicapped by mental retardation, cerebral palsy, autism, or epilepsy. Although the legislative definition uses these four medical conditions as examples, the underlying concept of developmental disabilities is that all individuals who are disabled early in life by substantial lifelong handicaps have common needs for special services. At some time services must be focused on an individual's unique needs and abilities and not based on expectations implied by a diagnostic label; a common diagnosis does not necessarily mean identical needs. Finally, those most in need of this individual focus are people who have been neglected in the past because they have a combination of disabling conditions and do not fit neatly into any one diagnostic category. Anyone interested in the field of developmental disabilities should both understand this underlying philosophy and have some basic knowledge about the individual handicapping conditions included. This chapter focuses on the four primary handicaps that comprise developmental disabilities: mental retardation, cerebral palsy, autism, and epilepsy.

MENTAL RETARDATION

Mental retardation is a descriptive term applied to those individuals who develop intellectually at below average rates and experience unusual difficulties in learning, social adjustment, and economic productivity. However, this label covers a broad spectrum of capabilities, and to consider a stereotyped image of a mentally retarded person is as invalid as suggesting a stereotype for those people classified as normal.

This chapter is an edited version of the narrative portion of a slide/tape presentation produced by the National Foundation of Dentistry and the Developmental Disabilities Technical Assistance System.

The vast majority of mentally retarded individuals are mildly or moderately disabled. They often attend special education classes as children and enter the job force as adults, either in sheltered or independent working environments. Only a small percentage of mentally retarded people are profoundly disabled and require extensive assistance in daily life.

Some of the major causes of retardation include prenatal infection in the mother, such as rubella; intoxication, such as lead poisoning; metabolic, growth, and nutritional problems; and cultural deprivation.

More than 6 million individuals are believed to be mentally retarded. More than 100,000 babies born each year are likely to join this group, unless far-reaching preventive measures can be discovered and employed. One out of every 10 Americans has a mentally retarded person in the family.

However, the mentally retarded individual is a person—not a statistic.

Despite the many obstacles that mentally retarded individuals face in our competitive society, they and their families often succeed in changing struggle into triumph. The determination exerted by many retarded people, coupled with advancements in the field of human services, means that *fewer* of them are warehoused today in large state institutions, forced to sit out their days on benches or to do menial work without pay.

In addition to the positive changes taking place in some institutions, programs in the community are reflecting a greater sensitivity by our society to the fact that although one may be mentally retarded, that disability does not diminish his basic humanity and possibilities. Mentally retarded children are gaining greater access to educational opportunities at early ages and the implications will be realized as they grow into adulthood. Just as education for the normal child is directed at providing experiences that will allow him to cope in society, so too education for the mentally retarded person is aimed at helping him to enter a real world. The intent is to prepare each child for the highest level of self-sufficiency. Although real equal opportunity for a public education is still wanting in many communities, advancements have been achieved due to the efforts of many dedicated advocacy organizations and families of retarded people. Such opportunity must continue, from preschool through vocational training for adults. Sheltered workshops serve as both training centers, for those able to assume competitive jobs, and long-term vocational centers, for those who need a more protective working environment. At such centers, dedicated staffs break down tasks into their most basic components so that many products needed by industry can be produced on a subcontractual basis. The utensils you use on your next airline flight may have been packaged in a sheltered workshop, as might the instructions included with medications you take. Perhaps a mentally retarded person cleaned the reprocessed components in your telephone.

Alternative forms of sheltered employment are also developing: the Pride

Pet Palace in Denver is an example. Retarded people are able to develop retail skills as well as learn to care for animals dependent on *them*.

The financial compensation provided by sheltered employment is usually minimal—typically $100 per month. Jobs held in the competitive market pay better, but often retarded individuals receive minimum wage at best. Because income largely determines one's level of independence and quality of housing, limited employment opportunities and inadequate wages tend to be accompanied with substandard housing for many retarded people. A concerted effort is now being made to establish small group homes located in the community. If zoning laws are not used as tools to discriminate, more group homes can be located in areas of cities other than crime-ridden neighborhoods. With broader options, fewer individuals will be forced to live in nursing homes and institutions because there is no other place for them.

Persons with mental retardation pursue all types of unstructured and highly individual life-styles. To see someone of this minority swinging in the park, standing in a grocery line, or having a taco for lunch is not uncommon. Recreation is often a vital part of their lives. The most organized effort in this regard is the Special Olympics, a program in which developmentally disabled individuals compete with one another in track and field events, swimming, bowling, and most recently skiing. There are also recreational clubs for weekend and evening activities. The pleasure expressed on such occasions is evidence that the sensitivity of society can be transformed into significant and humane progress.

CEREBRAL PALSY

Cerebral palsy is a developmental disability that can mask a capable individual behind severe and outwardly distracting motor dysfunction. An alert and well-functioning mind can be obscured by a body that will not allow controlled movement or easily understandable speech. A person with cerebral palsy may experience intense frustration because of his inability to inform people of his true identity.

An estimated 750,000 individuals with cerebral palsy live in the United States. As with mental retardation, many of the causes of cerebral palsy are associated with prenatal and perinatal problems, such as prematurity, lack of oxygen to the newborn during birth, infection, or a blow to the head. Perhaps as many as three-quarters of all persons with cerebral palsy have additional disabilities, such as retardation, seizures, auditory and visual handicaps, or communication disorders.

Educators in schools serving the cerebral palsied must be complemented by physical and occupational therapists, speech therapists, audiologists, and others in order to address needs in an interdisciplinary manner. While the intellectual potential of the child is being maximized, muscles can be stretched and exercised and speech skills developed. If no sensory handicap is an impediment, cerebral palsied children with normal or near normal intelligence can absorb education in the ordinary manner, and as they do, the unaffected centers of the brain can develop so that their influence over the damaged controls becomes more effective. Speech improvement can result, as well as fewer purposeless movements of the limbs. The need for education is equally great for those cerebral palsied individuals who are also mentally retarded. Special attention is required to enable these children to cope with their disabilities and to help them reach their full potential.

Residential needs of cerebral palsied individuals are varied in accordance with the severity of the handicap, age, intelligence, and ability to act on one's own behalf. If a protective environment is needed, residential facilities are available, which range from large institutions, to nursing homes, to small group homes, to apartments. In any case, the residence should suit the individual's needs. Many cerebral palsied individuals whose level of ability and possibilities far exceed their need for custodial care are living in institutions because there are no other available alternatives. The same is true for some residents of nursing homes, particularly young adults who are surrounded by sick and elderly people. Many cerebral palsied persons are capable of living totally independently in the community, and may be married, but often face architectural or financial barriers to good housing. Moreover, financial barriers exist that prevent the purchase and maintenance of group homes for persons with cerebral palsy.

Architectural and transportation barriers restrict access to employment as well. Those obstacles can magnify themselves and create economic hardships. After all, a person cannot go around knocking on doors to get in if he cannot even get to the door.

Employment in the mainstream depends upon the level of skills a person has, but the actual procurement of a job also depends upon the attitudes of employers. Many cerebral palsied people have demonstrated beyond a doubt that they can produce effectively if given equal opportunities. Simply stated, cerebral palsied people are labeled and diagnosed, and too frequently are not perceived as capable human beings.

Cerebral palsied persons, as is true of all disabled people, are more like others than they are different from them. Yet the differences between them and the nondisabled population are so often emphasized that they overshadow the individual capabilities of a person with cerebral palsy. The future of all developmentally disabled individuals will be determined by the amount of thoughtful and serious care given by our society to identification and early care of high risk infants, improved access to education and vocational training, removal of architectural and transportation barriers, long-term care, deinstitutionalization, and institutional reform.

AUTISM

Autism is one of the most baffling and distressing disabilities of childhood. The word *autism* comes from the Greek word *autos*, meaning self. This term was chosen because these children's aloof, withdrawn personalities cause them to appear to be living in a private, inaccessible dream world—isolated, seemingly by choice, from contact with others.

In the United States there are roughly 60,000 autistic children under 18 years of age. Boys are affected three or four times more often than girls.

Contrary to a widespread misconception, autism is *not* a result of bad parenting. It is now considered to be a neuro-integrative disorder. The brain is not functioning in a well-organized manner. The autistic child cannot respond appropriately to the environment. He can see; he can hear; he can tell when he is being touched, but often he cannot attribute accurate meaning to that sensory stimulation.

Exactly where and when the children's difficulties in understanding begin is not yet known. Sometimes retardation, or seizures, or another associated disability further confuse accurate diagnosis. Many problems are still unsolved, but it is possible to describe how an autistic child behaves and how he can be helped.

Some autistic children are model babies, not even crying when they are hungry. Others behave in exactly the opposite way. Both kinds of babies are difficult and unrewarding for parents.

Even if the parents have not worried about their child during the baby stage, when he reaches his second year the problems become obvious. He does not begin to talk at the expected time, and he begins to be frustrated by his handicaps. Autistic children usually have to make a long, painful effort before putting a few words together. Some never talk at all.

A young autistic child often seems to respond oddly to the things he sees and hears. He is liable to be frightened of quite harmless things, and yet he ignores real dangers. One mother reported the following about her child:

> He loves horses, he always has. When he was real little he used to frighten me because he had no fear of them at all; he would go hang on their tails or swing under their legs. They didn't kick him at all. I know if it had been anyone else they would have. But Richard seemed to be able to get away with these things. He would sit on the fence for hours and watch them.

Some autistic children do not seem to notice pain, but as they grow older they may become sensitive to discomfort. Children with these handicaps have many behavior problems. The saddest aspect for parents is that their child seems to be indifferent to them in his early years. He appears to be unaware of the existence of anyone else at all. As they very slowly learn to speak and understand language, they can become friendly and sociable. Some autistic children eventually become quite cheerful and extroverted, although their handicaps tend to prevent the development of truly adult and mature relationships with other people.

Fairly uncommon are cases of autistic children who are outstandingly gifted in some way. Some can play musical instruments or compose tunes, or calculate long sums in their heads with great speed and accuracy. Unfortunately, even these specially gifted children are often unable to manage the ordinary affairs of life and need someone to help them organize their lives.

At present, few communities or states offer appropriate services of any kind for the autistic child. One parent reported:

> When it came time to put him in school or when it came time that I decided that he must go to school, I found out that the local school was not equipped for this kind of problem. There wasn't a school in the whole state of Colorado. So I went to the Joint Budget Committee and asked for my tax money back because he was not receiving an education like all the other kids in Colorado and somebody must be using his money. I went to the governor and told him that I had been to every one of the agencies and none of them could help me. They all agreed that I had a problem, they all felt sorry for me and wished they could help; but they all referred me to someone else who referred me back to them. Being the governor you must be the end of the line, so please tell me what we can do about this. Within a couple of weeks they had established a task force to look into the problem of autism and this is how our first public school program got started.

When services are available, they frequently can only help a fraction of the children needing assistance.

When autistic children cannot live at home, special residential schools may solve the problem, but very few places are available and the costs are extremely high. Some states will provide either partial or total payment of tuition so that such children can attend private residential schools when necessary. Other autistic children may end up in large institutions where no special programs are available.

Although some autistic adults may be able to earn their living at a job in the mainstream, most require sheltered work. However, few such programs have been developed, because in the past, autistic children were likely to have been misdiagnosed as having untreatable mental retardation and were lost in institutions. If autistic children are to become even partially self-sufficient as adults, more vocational training must be available.

Residential programs, such as group and satellite homes and apartments, are needed for autistic adults who no longer have a family home.

Many people are trying to find ways of helping autistic children. To date, no single approach seems to provide the perfect answer.

EPILEPSY

There is no explanation why brain cells discharge abnormally and cause epileptic seizures. Similar to the other disabilities, seizures are related to infection, allergy, and toxic substances. Birth problems, including lack of oxygen and traumatic head injury, may also lead to seizures, which may range from total lapses of consciousness to brief disturbances involving only one part of the body. One person in 50—approximately 4 million Americans— probably has some form of epilepsy. Epilepsy can happen to anyone, at any age, at any time. It cannot be cured. However, through the use of anticonvulsant medication, seizures can be *controlled* in an estimated 80% of all cases. What medication cannot control is the public's attitude toward epileptic seizures.

Finding employment is the biggest single problem faced by persons with epilepsy; they experience an estimated unemployment rate of between 15% and 25%—approximately 100,000 to 200,000 men and women. The primary cause of this alarmingly high figure is society's misunderstanding and fear.

The *fact* is that the seizures of most people with epilepsy are controlled through medication, and even when a seizure occurs, it is momentary and does not impair ability to function once the seizure is over. Denial of equal opportunity to employment, then, creates a whole set of economic handicaps far greater than the restrictions of the disability itself. Access to health insurance and drivers' licenses are other obstacles for some individuals, regardless of the severity of their disability.

When discrimination does not stand in their way, people with epilepsy are fully capable of living independent, active, productive lives.

CONCLUSION

Mental retardation, cerebral palsy, autism, and epilepsy: these four diagnostic categories are developmental disabilities. "Developmental disabilities" is more than a list of handicapping conditions; it is a concept presenting these challenges: a challenge to develop a humane and comprehensive system of residential, educational, and vocational services, transportation, recreation, and social opportunities; a challenge to fully develop individual human potential.

3

Developmentally Disabled Persons: Their Rights and Their Needs for Services

Sondra Diamond

BILL OF RIGHTS FOR THE DISABLED*

We, the disabled, being entitled to the same rights as any other citizen, do hereby claim these rights. The universality of man is such that all people are not created physically equal, but we are created equal in our needs to live a full and meaningful life and in our right to pursue it.

Herewith are the rights to which we are entitled:

1. THE RIGHT TO AN EDUCATION
   To be able to attend both private and public schools in the primary and secondary grades and college
2. THE RIGHT TO NONDISCRIMINATING ACCESS TO PUBLIC ACCOMMODATIONS
   To gain entrance into a public accommodation without embarrassment or inconvenience
3. THE RIGHT OF ACCESS WITHOUT ARCHITECTURAL BAR-RIERS INTO PUBLIC ACCOMMODATIONS
   To be able to enter and fully utilize any building, be it built with public or private monies
4. THE RIGHT TO NONDISCRIMINATING SERVICE IN PUBLIC ACCOMMODATIONS
   To be able to receive equal treatment when a service is being rendered
5. THE RIGHT TO TRAVEL WHETHER ESCORTED OR UNES-CORTED
   To be able, on one's own responsibility, to fully utilize airplanes, trains, buses, and taxi cabs
6. THE RIGHTS TO ANY LICENSING AS ACCORDED TO ALL CITIZENS
   To be able to receive a license from any government agency without having to fulfill special requirements because of a disability

---

*Copyrighted by the author.

7. THE RIGHT TO GAINFUL EMPLOYMENT AS AN EMPLOYEE OR ENTREPRENEUR
   To be able to obtain a competitive position in Civil Service or private enterprise, and, if self-employed, all the inherent rights
8. THE RIGHT TO RENT OR PURCHASE ANY HOUSING FACILITY
   To be able to obtain a mortgage or sign a lease on one's own responsibility, be it in public or private housing
9. THE RIGHT TO FULL AND EQUAL MEDICAL CARE
   To be able to receive equal treatment by doctors and hospitals and to have confidence that they will have knowledge and understanding of our disabilities
10. THE RIGHT TO ECONOMIC, SOCIAL, AND POLITICAL INDEPENDENCE
    To be able to feel assured that all individuals to whom we relate will look upon us as capable citizens

In looking back over my life, for the purpose of determining the types of services that I needed and wanted, I feel that the place to begin is with the Bill of Rights for the Disabled, which I wrote in 1972. The Bill of Rights for the Disabled was written to illustrate the kinds of services and programs that would have enhanced my development and normalized my present and future.

The agencies that worked with me worked diligently to facilitate my habilitation, in order for me to be able to travel and function in society. Their focus was maximizing my abilities without taking into account the barriers that society put up. Their role instead should have been a dual one: maximizing my potential and minimizing society's obstacles—philosophical, attitudinal, and architectural. To habilitate or rehabilitate only, without changing the environment, negates the gains, both psychological and physical, that the individual makes; the frustrations that are met turn the habilitation process into a farce.

The history of the Bill of Rights speaks for itself.

THE RIGHT TO AN EDUCATION

Historically, physically disabled persons have been segregated into separate schools, particularly in the first and second grades. Large metropolitan cities, such as Philadelphia, usually have one public school for the physically disabled that can accommodate a few hundred students. However, such public schools, due to space shortage, are very selective in the children that they accept, favoring children with higher intelligence quotients and less severe disabilities. The children that are not accepted into these schools are given a home education sponsored by the Board of Education, are forced into expensive private schools, or receive no education at all. Ten percent of the population is identified as physically disabled. Clearly, existing public schools or home programs cannot accommodate all disabled children.

The result of a segregated education for the disabled child is twofold: first, the disabled child is isolated and becomes socially and psychologically immature as a result of being deprived of the life-enriching experiences to which his nondisabled peers are exposed; second, as a result of this segregation, the fears and prejudices of the nondisabled toward the disabled are perpetuated.

Special schools for disabled children, aside from an educational curriculum, also provide rehabilitation services, such as physical and occupational therapy. Although the school day is the same length as that of the nondisabled child, the time allotted for education is not equal to that allotted for a nondisabled child.

As a student about to enter high school, I wanted to go to a mainstream (nonspecial) high school, because I felt that I would need the education and experiences in order to be prepared for college. I was not permitted to attend a mainstream high school because of the severity of my disability. It is ironic that even as a child I realized the importance of these experiences, and in retrospect I found the transition I had to make from special school to college a monumental one. Adjustment to peer groups, adhering to time schedules, and the need for greater physical independence were just a few of the new problems with which I was faced.

THE RIGHT TO NONDISCRIMINATING ACCESS TO PUBLIC ACCOMMODATIONS

I have been asked to leave many theatres and restaurants. The Fair Practices Ordinance of Philadelphia has been amended to read:

> It shall be unlawful public accommodation practice to refuse, withhold from or deny to any person because of his race, color, religion, national origin, ancestry or physical handicap, either directly or indirectly, any of the accommodations, advantages, facilities or privileges of such place of public accommodation, resort or amusement.

Why must there be laws declaring that to deny a disabled person access is illegal? Recently, a friend of mine in a wheelchair was thrown out of a gift shop outside the city limits of Philadelphia. She contacted the Commission on Human Relations of Philadelphia, which administers and enforces the Fair Practices Ordinance. She also contacted the American Civil Liberties Union. She was told that, in her county, the shop's action was legal. She was told that she could not sue the store, even though she had been subjected to great indignities.

THE RIGHT OF ACCESS WITHOUT
ARCHITECTURAL BARRIERS INTO PUBLIC ACCOMMODATIONS

This right can best be understood through empathizing with an experience that I had that, in retrospect, is humorous, but at the time was not.

It was 2:00 A.M. I was alone in a Chicago hotel room feeling no pain as a result of too many drinks, and Mother Nature was insistently making me aware that my bladder was full. Not a unique or unsolvable problem under ordinary circumstances, but I could not get my wheelchair into the bathroom; the door was too narrow. I had been sent to this Chicago convention by the United Cerebral Palsy Association. This being my first day, I had been busy with meetings and conferences, using the bathroom facilities everywhere except in my hotel room—until 2:00 A.M., that is.

Of course, I had written to the hotel weeks in advance, explaining my disability and describing my needs in terms of the dimensions of the room and bathroom. I received a letter of confirmation stating that I could have what I requested.

Tears of pain and frustration were streaming down my face. I was too embarrassed, both over my drunkenness and my inability to attend to my personal needs, to call another conventioneer. It occurred to me that there must be a hotel service for such problems. There was a bar, a hairdresser, a restaurant; surely, I thought, someone must be available in this hotel to help relieve this bodily need!

I wheeled myself to the telephone and looked at the outer dial around the numbers. Corresponding to each number on the dial there was a hotel service. As I frantically glanced around the dial, "housekeeper," "laundry," "doctor" flashed before my eyes, but none of these was what I was looking for. I looked again and "carpenter" stood out in vibrating three dimensions.

I dialed the number and this is what transpired: "This is Miss Diamond in Room 809. I am in a wheelchair and would like to go to the bathroom; however, I cannot fit through the door." The deep male voice at the other end said, "Are you drunk, lady?" "Yes, I am, but that's not relevant at the moment. The point is, I want you to come up to my room and remove the bathroom door." The faceless carpenter said, "You mean, remove the door from its hinges?" "Exactly," said I, "now we're understanding each other!"

I had come a long way in my struggle for independence. The man at the other end of the phone was to decide whether or not I would overcome this obstacle and be independent this night. "It's 2:00 A.M., lady! You want me to come up now?" "Either you come or I'll have to call the housekeeping department to repair the consequences of your absence!" I was beginning to picture a maid with a mop and bucket coming up to my room in 15 minutes: that was my only alternative if this carpenter wouldn't cooperate. My carpenter said, "Okay, lady," and abruptly hung up. I didn't know whether he was coming or not, but I decided to give him a few minutes to digest our conversation. My pride and fate were in his hands.

Fifteen minutes later there was a heavy knock at the door. As I opened it, a man dressed in overalls and carrying a tool box asked, "You wanted your toilet door removed, lady?" "Yes, please come in!" Within 5 minutes, the door was off its hinges and the carpenter stood before me asking, "Where shall I put it lady?" He had called me a lady, so I choked down my impulse to tell him "where to put it" and suggested instead that he stand it in the corner. Before I could hand the carpenter a tip for his services, he packed up his tools and was halfway out the door. I tried to give him something, but he waved my hand away and quickly retreated, slamming the door behind him.

THE RIGHT TO NONDISCRIMINATING SERVICE IN PUBLIC ACCOMMODATIONS

While shopping, I have often been followed around by a salesperson and watched very carefully. If I ask to purchase an item, it is often suggested that I look at the less expensive products. In department stores, I am frequently directed to bargain basements. If I am with a friend, the following dialogue ensues:

> "I am looking for an evening dress," I say.
> "What size does she want?" the saleslady says to my companion.
> "I would like a size 12," I say.
> "What color does she want?" the salesperson asks my companion.

And so it goes, with me talking to the salesperson and the salesperson talking to my companion. Slowly I fade into the role of nonperson.

While dining out, in most restaurants not only am I not given a menu, but once I secure one, I am not given the courtesy of being spoken to by the waiter or waitress. My friends are invariably asked, "What does she want to eat?" Despite my disability, I have been taught how to speak, how to read, and how to make appropriate decisions. Why?

THE RIGHT TO TRAVEL WHETHER ESCORTED OR UNESCORTED

The right to travel is one of the greatest problems of the physically disabled because, by virtue of our disabilities, our mobility is limited. Society adds to the handicap when it imposes restrictions on the freedom of travel.

For example, a Civil Aeronautics Board ruling formerly stated that a disabled person may not travel on a commercial carrier unless accompanied by a nonhandicapped attendant. Flying is the most comfortable and physically practical way for disabled people to travel long distances. This activity served as a restriction from utilizing public conveyances. The additional expense of an attendant for air travel and for taxis as a result of buses being inaccessible was costly and handicapped our mobility. Fortunately the attendant requirement has been changed by regulation, but the right to travel remains a primary concern of handicapped persons.

THE RIGHTS TO ANY LICENSING AS ACCORDED ALL CITIZENS

When physically disabled people apply for drivers' licenses, they are subjected to rigorous physical examinations, and the test for licensing is an extremely lengthy one. In most cases, the applicant must return at least two or three times before being granted a license. In many instances, he is not granted a license to drive, and frequently is forced to get a license in another state. Disabled drivers have an excellent safety record and yet the reason for not granting licenses is usually that they will be "menaces on the road."

The same demeaning treatment occurs when physically disabled individuals apply for marriage licenses. Many personal and potentially embarrassing questions are asked of the person applying for the license and, in many instances, letters from physicians are required attesting to the fact that the individual may marry.

Several years ago I applied for a State Fishing License. I was denied the license because I was not in a state tubercular institution or mental institution and only patients in those institutions were granted *free* licenses. When I explained that I did not want a free license, but wanted to pay for one, I was still viewed as a "patient," but one for whom they did not have a category.

Again, the role of rehabilitation agencies must go beyond dealing with individuals with disabilities and extend to intensive public awareness programs, the targets being State Licensing Bureaus and other governmental agencies.

THE RIGHT TO GAINFUL EMPLOYMENT
AS AN EMPLOYEE OR ENTREPRENEUR

There are 60,000 paraplegics of working age in this country; more than 50% of them are unemployed. There are 400,000 people of working age with epilepsy in this country; more than 25% of them are unemployed. There are 150,000 blind people of working age in this country; more than 66% are unemployed. There are 200,000 people of working age in this country with cerebral palsy; more than 90% of them are unemployed. According to a Social Security Administration survey, there are 12 million physically disabled

Americans capable of full-time employment. Sixty-four percent of them are unemployed.

A Prentice-Hall Company study[1] indicated that the absenteeism, lateness, and job turnover rates for the disabled are lower than for the nondisabled, and that dependability and morale were higher for the disabled. Two interesting facts resulted from a Labor Department comparison of work records for 11,000 disabled and 18,000 nondisabled employees. Disabled workers had 6% fewer on-the-job injuries, and out-produced the nondisabled by a ratio of 101 to 111. What of the physically disabled who are employed? The median income for the disabled is $3,000 a year. Although they out-produce, are more reliable, and are less accident-prone than nondisabled persons, they are forced to earn less.

Two states, Iowa and New Jersey, have made it unlawful to discriminate against the physically disabled in employment practices. The fact that laws have to be made to protect the disabled proves that we are a valid minority group. Laws that inhibit the disabled, such as the Civil Aeronautics Board ruling mentioned earlier, further validate the minority group concept. However, this is a piecemeal approach. The only answer is to amend the Civil Rights Act of 1964 to make it unlawful to discriminate against individuals who are physically handicapped because of such handicaps. H.R. 2658 supports this amendment. If this bill is passed, the physically disabled will be able to compete for the jobs they have been or can be trained for. It is incumbent upon the agencies that work with the disabled to support this bill in order to make their direct client work more meaningful.

My professional career as a counseling psychologist in private practice was born out of many frustrating months of job-seeking after acquiring bachelor's and master's degrees. Career counseling for the disabled has been a long-neglected area. For instance, the counseling that I received both in high school and college emphasized that I sit back and appreciate my education for its own sake and not seek employment. Counseling services and employment services that are available to the nondisabled are not architecturally or attitudinally available to the disabled. Specialized agencies that work with the disabled often lose sight of this fact. They assume that the disabled can make use of the aforementioned services, and therefore see no need to provide these services themselves.

Private practice, for me, was initially a compromise; my primary goal was to work in a setting with other professional people. I also wanted the job security and all of the benefits that accompany being an employee. Prospec-

---

[1] *The Disabled in Action of Pennsylvania*. Personal communication to Honorable Carl Perkins, Chairman of the Committee on Education and Labor. April 28, 1973.

tive employers that interviewed me were blunt in their rejection. They said that if they hired me I would "ugly up" the place, or their clients would need more help after seeing me than when they came for counseling services. Some, although patronizing, acknowledged my education and intellect, while others treated me as if I were retarded.

The rejection experiences left me with a battered ego, which resulted in a period of pajama-clad self-pity that lasted for months. From this evolved the decision to go into private practice, because the only other way to go was down.

THE RIGHT TO RENT OR PURCHASE ANY HOUSING FACILITY

An obvious right, you might say. But why has it been necessary for a Commission on Human Relations of a large city to amend its fair practices ordinance to read as follows?

> It shall be an unlawful housing practice for the owner of any commercial housing, or any other real property hereof, to refuse to sell, rent, lease, or in any way discriminate because of race, color, religion, national origin, ancestry, or physical handicap in the terms, conditions, or privileges of the sale, rental or lease of any commercial housing accommodations or other real property or in the furnishing of facilities in connection therewith.

The amendment goes on to say:

> It shall be unlawful for any lending institution to discriminate against any person because of a physical handicap of such person in lending, guaranteeing loans, accepting mortgages or otherwise making available funds for the purchase, acquisition, construction, rehabilitation, repair, or maintenance of any housing accommodation.

Apparently, legal action may be necessary to allow the physically handicapped to live where they choose.

THE RIGHT TO FULL AND EQUAL MEDICAL CARE

Unequal medical care affects three types of hospitalized physically disabled people: the newborn infant who is born with a physical disability; the physically disabled individual who is hospitalized for a medical condition other than his disability; and an individual who incurs a disability in adulthood.

A newborn infant who will be permanently disabled, but who will survive if medical treatment is administered, is often not protected by the law as are other infants. If a nondisabled baby is born requiring medical treatment and the parents of that child, either for religious or other reasons, do not wish the child to be treated, the attending physicians will get a court order to protect the child. This has rarely been true in cases of children born with birth defects.

This reflects a belief, held by some people, that there is no point in attempting to prolong the life of a child who would be disabled anyway.

When a physically disabled person is hospitalized for a condition related to his disability, the nursing staff and technicians are usually aware of his special needs. When he is hospitalized for something other than his disability, it's a different story. In my adult life, I have been hospitalized for medical problems other than my disability and have suffered undue pain and anguish through lack of understanding and knowledge of the medical personnel.

There may be differences in the care required by the disabled versus the nondisabled when they are hospitalized; these differences may not be perceived by hospital staff unprepared to cope with them. The disabled often cannot care for their personal needs, such as toileting and dressing. The disabled frequently cannot be given tests, such as x-rays and blood tests, in the same way as other patients. Medication must be administered in many different ways depending on the patient's disability. Medical personnel are not given training in how to handle the special needs of the disabled.

Agencies that work with the disabled can attack this problem in many ways. One way would be to institute courses in nursing schools and medical schools to help the students learn about the individual problems of the disabled. Another way would be to conduct inservice training programs in hospitals to help the already-trained staff understand the problems of the disabled. A third service in dealing with the medical problems of the disabled would be to provide a liaison who could go with a disabled person to the hospital. The liaison would familiarize the immediate staff with the special problems and needs of the disabled patient.

Specialized medical personnel in dentistry, gynecology, and psychiatry need to be trained to work with the disabled and their unique problems. As grants and fellowships are awarded to eradicate or discover causes of disabilities, so should they be awarded to individuals who will work directly with the disabled in the previously mentioned fields.

The task of improving medical services for the disabled is multifaceted. It ranges from helping the disabled cope with a medical problem, in view of the fact that this compounds the already existing problem of a poor body image, to educating those in medicine.

THE RIGHT TO ECONOMIC, SOCIAL, AND POLITICAL INDEPENDENCE

Many of the rights that are denied the disabled, and the services that are needed, can be summed up in the phrase "economic, social, and political independence." One of many examples is the difficulty that the disabled person has in purchasing both health and automobile insurance. The myth that a physically disabled person is "sick" is prevalent among health insurance companies; such archaic thinking often colors a decision not to sell health insurance to the physically disabled. Automobile insurance, if purchasable at all by the physically disabled, is much more expensive than for the nondisabled. This is unjust in view of the higher safety record of the disabled compared to the nondisabled driver.

Another example is the way in which the physically disabled are disenfranchised. Architecturally inaccessible polling places make it impossible for the minority voice of the disabled to be heard. When this issue is raised, the absentee ballot is pointed to as a satisfactory solution. However, the system of absentee voting has three basic flaws. In order for a disabled person to obtain an absentee ballot, he must show proof from a physician that he is unable to get to a polling place; second, an absentee ballot must be submitted well in advance of the date on which everyone else votes, denying the disabled the right to hear the issues up until the last moment; and finally, an absentee ballot must be applied for before each primary or general election. Therefore, each time a disabled individual wishes to vote, he must go through the tedious task of obtaining a letter from a doctor and reapplying for an absentee ballot.

Because the disabled are not seen as complete people, a dearth of psychological services exists. This is particularly unfortunate in that, aside from the usual psychological problems that human beings must confront, the disabled are faced with unique psychological problems arising from dealing with and adjusting to a disability. These unique problems are myriad: the universal need for "private space" (the unseen boundary around our body which we do not want invaded by touch or look unless we give out tacit approval), the recurrent periods of self-pity that are born out of the conflicts that we experience as a result of what we want to do, what we are capable of doing, and what we are permitted to do; and the distorted self-image that arises out of the conflict between the way a disabled person sees himself and the way others relate to him.

A final, but certainly not unimportant, example of how we are not able to fully attain social independence is the lack of sex education and counseling for the disabled. People seem to feel, falsely, that the less a disabled person knows about sex, the less likely it is that he will be sexually irresponsible. Furthermore, doesn't the disabled person have enough trouble learning how to read or feed himself? Why should we worry him about sex? A disabled person has the same physical and emotional needs as everyone else. He experiences the same anxieties during adolescence through the need for sex role identification and control of sexual impulses. A disabled person has the same need for affection and the same hope for marriage and a family. Not only must we develop specially trained personnel to educate and counsel the disabled concerning their sexual needs, but we must sensitize so-called "unqualified"

people, such as doctors, nurses, or teachers, to help the disa
their sexual needs.

Finally, the freedom and independence of disabled people ....uted, in large measure, by the ways in which people respond to our "differentness." From childhood on, we are taught a set of attitudes toward people who are different from ourselves, whether they be of a different race, nationality, sex, or physical disability. In the case of the physically disabled, we are taught not to stare and not to be rude. We are left with a very confused set of feelings. These feelings cannot be ignored: they must be faced if we are to recognize the problems of the physically disabled.

Information is readily available concerning different types of handicapping conditions, rehabilitation techniques, and seemingly isolated problems like employment, transportation, and the psychosocial problems of the disabled. The area of education that will be most neglected concerns subjective feelings that confront a person in dealing with the physically disabled. Examine your feelings. Examine them in terms of what you were taught about the disabled when you were growing up. Examine your feelings about the disabled in terms of your own fears, your self-doubts, and your self-concepts about *your* body image.

CONCLUSION

There must be a realization that rehabilitation services are not enough. A disabled person lives in a real world. Not only must he be taught how to care for himself, but he must also learn how to live in a society that is not tailored to the problems of the disabled. Agencies must strive toward this end, and in doing so must take on the role of advocate. The role of advocacy is a dual one. First, the disabled individual must be assisted in every way possible to fully actualize his potential. This advocacy role should be viewed as a temporary one with the goal of independence ever in mind. Additionally, the advocacy role is one in which agencies must actively participate in changing how society feels about the disabled. Through promoting public awareness, as well as helping to revamp the legal structure to accommodate the disabled, agencies can genuinely advocate in the best interests of their disabled clients.

4

The Developmental Disabilities Council and Its Membership

Gary Richman and Paula Breen

The heart of the developmental disabilities concept is the DD Council, a broadly conceived partnership that reaches out across state government departments and beyond to embrace private professionals providing services to the developmentally disabled and consumers of services or their representatives. This chapter traces the evolution of the DD Council as articulated in federal law, regulations, and policy.

The Developmental Disabilities Services and Facilities Construction Act (PL 91-517) of 1970 and federal regulations that support it were primarily concerned with setting minimum levels of compliance. They detail the least that the state and DD Council must do in order to participate in the formula grant program—that is, to receive their share of the appropriated federal funds.

The 1975 legislation, the Developmentally Disabled Assistance and Bill of Rights Act (PL 94-103), had a major impact on the DD Council and how it functions. Although this impact included many new responsibilities, it was not a new direction; rather it was a more explicit expression of the long-standing congressional intent for the DD program. The first law had been intentionally vague in its language in order to allow creativity and flexibility in the states' implementation of the DD program. Congress had more than 3 years to watch and evaluate the DD program and how it functioned in the states. The House of Representatives proposed to continue the vague and flexible approach. The Senate, conversely, proposed a very specific and directive intent of Congress: Public Law 94-103 was a compromise between these two approaches.

In 1978, after 3 more years of experience with the DD program, Congress again made changes in the law. The latest legislation, PL 95-602, marks some significant new directions for DD Councils and the DD program.

COUNCIL MEMBERSHIP

The 1970 act required each state and territory to designate or form a "State Planning and Advisory Council" in order to participate in the DD program. Either a newly formed body or the designation of an existing state council or agency was permitted by the regulations so long as the other requirements were met. Among the "other requirements" specified in the original legislation and expanded by regulations and subsequent legislation is the composition of the Council. The 1970 DD act specifies the inclusion of "representatives of each principal State agency . . . concerned with services for persons with developmental disabilities." At a minimum this included representatives of the following service systems (Federal Register, 1972):

Special education
Vocational rehabilitation
Residential services for mentally retarded persons
Social services for the disabled and for families and children
Diagnostic and treatment services for crippled and/or retarded children
Health services or long-term care programs for adults with chronic neurological disorders (such as epilepsy and cerebral palsy)
Medical assistance

The January, 1977, regulations altered the list some; they specified that at least representatives of the following principal federal/state programs be included as state agency members of the Developmental Disabilities Council (Federal Register, 1977):

Education of the handicapped
Vocational rehabilitation
Public assistance
Medical assistance
Social services
Maternal and child health
Crippled children's services
Comprehensive health planning
Mental health

A second group also must be represented on each state DD Council: "representatives of local agencies and nongovernmental organizations and groups concerned with services for persons with developmental disabilities."

The 1978 law adds representatives of "higher education training facilities" to this group. This second group is often referred to in a shorthand way as "private professionals" or "private providers of services."

Consumers or their representatives are the final group mandated by law to be on state DD Councils. The 1970 act required that they make up no less than one-third of the Council. Neither the original DD act nor the initial regulations clearly defined "customer." However, the regulations suggested that it could include persons with developmental disabilities and representatives of parent organizations. Persons "whose major occupation is either the administration of activities or the provision of services" cannot be counted as consumer members of DD Councils. This regulation tends to reinforce the logical notion that "providers" and "consumers" are mutually exclusive groups.

In the 1975 legislation and regulations the words *consumer* and *consumer representatives* were not used; instead there was a bit more specific information about who should and who should not make up this one-third of each Developmental Disabilities Council. The law specified that this one-third (which everyone still referred to as consumers or consumer reps) be comprised of persons with a developmental disability or their parents or guardians. Excluded from being counted in this one-third ("consumer representatives") were officers or employees of the entities or agencies that received Developmental Disabilities Council funds.

The 1978 legislation expanded the definition of the developmental disabilities target population and, in doing so, automatically broadened the scope of consumer membership on the Council. In addition, the new law expands the proportion of consumers from one-third to one-half of the full Council membership, one-third of which must be persons with developmental disabilities. The law goes on to require that at least one-third of the consumer members be immediate relatives or guardians of persons with "mentally impairing developmental disabilities" and that at least one member of this consumer subgroup must be an immediate relative or guardian of an institutionalized person with a developmental disability.

The original law called for each DD Council to be "adequately staffed." The 1972 regulations translated this to mean, at a minimum, "a full-time or part-time . . . planning director." By 1975, Congress was acutely aware of the need for DD Councils to have sufficient staff (and sufficient control over the staff) to meet its mandated responsibilities. The 1975 law called for the DD Council to have "adequate" personnel to ensure completion of the tasks, without defining "adequate." A controversial provision, which would have defined "adequate" as between 20% and 30% of the state's formula grant funds spent on staff, was deleted from the final version of the law. However, the conference report made a strong statement that it was the intent of Congress that DD Councils have meaningful staff support in order to carry out their responsibilites.

The 1977 regulations, which help to clarify the 1975 legislation and its intent, still did not tackle the definition of "adequate" but they did require that the staff "be responsible to the State Council." The 1978 legislation fails to improve on the ambiguous term *adequate*.

THE EVOLVING COUNCIL MANDATE

The initial DD legislation in 1970 said little beyond the levels of minimum compliance. By the lack of specificity the DD act encouraged flexibility and creative initiation on the part of each state and DD Council to work out patterns of organization and activity that were effective in their unique situation.

The 1975 legislation reflected Congressional desire to be more directive regarding the role of DD Councils. The 1975 law spelled out for the first time in the legislation the DD Councils' responsibilities. It called for the DD Councils to:

1. Supervise the development of and approve the State Plan
2. Monitor and evaluate the implementation of the State Plan
3. Have prior review and comment, to the maximum extent feasible, on all other State Plans that affect persons with developmental disabilities
4. Submit periodic reports to the Secretary of HEW through the governor

The consequence of the 1975 legislation being more directive was that the role of the DD Council was strengthened, with the emphasis placed on the Council's role as *planner, monitor, evaluator, and advocate*. In addition, specific attention to a number of program areas was required. Even the Council's official name was changed—the word *advisory* was deleted from the old title and it was designated a "State Planning Council." This symbolic strengthening of the Council role as planner was coupled with an explicit mandate to "serve as an advocate for persons with developmental disabilities." At the heart of this semantic jockeying was a certain tension between the administering agency of state government and the State Council members and staff over who calls the shots in writing the State DD Plan, shaping the DD program, and spending the DD dollars. The thrust of the 1975 act was to establish the DD Council as a separate entity with specified mandates and authority.

A significant characteristic of the 1978 legislation is that it puts the "brakes" on the development of DD Councils as independent, planning, and advocacy bodies with a panoramic perspective of all services needed by persons of any age with developmental disabilities. The latest legislation makes a number of significant changes in the Council's role:

1. The emphasis is again on "joint" development of the State Plan by the Council and the administering agency rather than a clear delineation of responsibility.
2. The commitment of a significant amount of DD funds is made to service provision as opposed to planning and advocacy functions of the Council.
3. The Council must, in effect, choose one or two of four specific age- and service-limited priority areas.

THE COUNCIL AND THE DESIGNATED STATE AGENCY

Since the beginning of the DD program, the DD acts and regulations have required that a state agency be designated (hence the shorthand term *designated state agency*) to administer or supervise the administration of the State Plan. There are provisions for splitting this responsibility among state agencies, but in practice this has been rare. The significance of the designated state agency is that it "administers" the DD Council and the monies that flow to the state under the DD act. The question of who has final authority over the use of that money, like the question of what constitutes adequate staff (with which it is frequently intertwined), has been answered differently in different states and in some cases has been a source of serious conflict between the DD Council and the state agency designated to "administer" it.

At the beginning of the DD program in the early 1970s, when the state DD money was often used to fund service projects, the question was one of grants management: Who reviews proposals and funding requests? Who decides the budget allocation? Some Councils were actively involved in grant-making decisions; others preferred to set general priorities for spending (e.g., services for young adults, group homes, advocacy) and allow the agency staff to review proposals and award funds within the Council's prescribed guidelines. The 1975 Senate Committee report made clear that the intent of Congress was that DD Councils should be concerned with setting priorities, direction, systems advocacy, and that administering agencies should handle "the burden of day to day administration of grants." The mechanism that Congress intended to be used by DD Councils and state agencies to clarify this division of labor was the design for implementation.

In essence, the design for implementation was the state agency's response to the goals and objectives specified by the DD Council. The Council had the rights of approval over the design for implementation and it became part of the State Plan submitted to HEW. The design for implementation reflected Congress's view of the Council and administrative agency having separate functions and being linked by a mechanism that required an active partnership. The 1978 legislation retreated from the attempt to define the relationship between the DD Council and their administering agency. The design for implementation has been omitted from the 1978 legislation and it is silent on the subject of the division of responsibility.

THE STATE PLAN

In simple terms, a State Plan is a "contract" between the state and the federal government. The federal government offers the state an amount of money provided it meets certain requirements. In the State Plan the state spells out how it will comply with those requirements. The State Plan is also the mechanism of accountability. The federal government uses the State Plan to hold the state accountable for such things as the type and quality of services to be provided to persons with developmental disabilities. This usually takes the form of minimum requirements or standards, which are the state's part of the "contract." The State Plan must in some form contain assurances that the state is indeed carrying out its part of the bargain.

The 1975 legislation made the State Plan a mechanism for guiding the focus of the DD Council and, to an extent, its method of operation. The intent of the legislation was to have DD Councils act as advocates and planners concerned with policy issues at the state level while not being concerned with the day-to-day administration of the service delivery system. In terms of operation this meant that the DD Council established the goals and objectives; was involved in gathering and analyzing data, including the prior review of State Plans affecting the developmentally disabled; and established and coordinated the procedures for planning, monitoring, and evaluating state programs. The DD Council had full approval power over the State Plan, which included how it was to be implemented—that is, how the DD funds and other resources were to be used in order to meet the goals and objectives set by the Council. The Council was further charged with monitoring the activities of the state to see that they were in compliance with the State Plan and its implementation design.

In 1975 the Senate gave extensive thought to the issue of the DD Council-state agency relationship. The Senate committee report on their version of the DD bill (S 462) described the nature of the relationship that Congress envisioned as a complementary, noncompetitive one. The committee report explained at some length Congress' expectation that DD Councils act in a "leadership and advocacy role" in the general direction and goals of the DD program while the state agency was assigned administrative responsibility for the implementation of the DD state plan with the concurrence of the

Council. The 1978 law simply calls for the DD Council and the agency to develop the plan jointly.

The 1978 legislation marked a shift in the evolution of the developmental disabilities program, and this is most evident in looking at the changing nature of the State Plan. In the earliest days of the DD program the State Plan was often viewed by the states as a perfunctory document prepared only to get the federal funds. Once the money was in hand it was generally distributed in grants for service programs. The State Plan requirements of the 1975 act and the accompanying regulations helped to give shape and substance to the philosophy of the DD program—that the role of the DD Council was to improve and expand services for persons of all ages with developmental disabilities by monitoring and influencing the existing human services systems in the state. Therefore the State Plan requirements in the 1975 act called on the Council to exercise planning, monitoring, evaluation, and advocacy skills. Some of its State Plan requirements included:

1. The description of the "quality, extent, and scope" of services provided or to be provided to persons with developmental disabilities within the state, including the prior review and comment on all State Plans with programs affecting the developmentally disabled. These other programs included:
   Education for the handicapped
   Vocational rehabilitation
   Public assistance
   Medical assistance
   Social services
   Maternal and child health
   Mental health and mental retardation
   Other related programs, such as aging
2. The setting and annual review of its goals, objectives, and priorities for the year. The 1975 legislation went on to direct the Council's attention to a number of specific areas to be *included among* the goals:
   a. The elimination of inappropriate placement of persons in institutions and the improvement of the quality of care and surroundings where institutional care is appropriate.
   b. The support for the establishment of community programs as alternatives to institutionalization.
   c. The provision for early screening, diagnosis, and evaluation.
   d. The provision for counseling, program coordination, follow-along services, protective services, and personal advocacy on behalf of developmentally disabled adults.
   e. The assurance that the human rights of all developmentally disabled

persons under the DD act are protected by three mechanisms: First, individual written habilitation plans to be prepared for all persons served under the DD act; second, an evaluation system based on individual progress; and third, a protection and advocacy system that is independent of any state agency that provides service or treatment.

These are just some of the 30 or more legislative requirements for the State Plan in 1975 law. These were broad requirements calling for the DD Councils to set goals and priorities in their planning and influencing activities. The councils were directed to pay particular attention to specific areas of concern, but the only fiscal restriction was that at least 10% of the FY 1976 formula grant and 30% for succeeding years be spent to implement the broad mandate of eliminating inappropriate institutionalization.

The 1978 act continues a trend that began in 1975 of focusing the Council attention on specific program areas. It goes further, however, and restricts the Council's field of action to any two (from a list of four) areas of the Council's choosing. Moreover, it shifts the main role of the Council from planning, influencing, and catalyzing the existing service systems to funding service programs. The 1978 legislation designates four priority service areas for council planning and program implementation:

1. Case management services to assist developmentally disabled persons in gaining access to needed services
2. Child development services, including early identification, diagnosis, evaluation and intervention, and the counseling and training of parents
3. Alternative community living arrangement services
4. Nonvocational social development services to improve daily living and work skills

The significant new feature of the 1978 law is that the council must select from this list of four priority service areas one or two priorities and must spend $100,000 or 65% of the formula grant allocation (whichever is greater) on providing services in its selected priority(ies) area. Should the federal appropriation for the DD formula grant program exceed $60 million nationally, the Council may select a maximum of three from the list of four priority areas. However, it still must spend $100,000 or 65% of its formula grant (whichever is greater) on service provision. Therefore, while much of the language of planning and even many of the State Plan requirements of the 1975 law survive in some form in the 1978 legislation, it is this new thrust of service provision in designated areas that moves to center stage in the DD program.

In part responding to and reflecting the views of those who have become impatient with "planning," Congress apparently hopes to speed the transition from planning to action at the state level. The broad areas defined as case management, child development, community living, and nonvocational development programs certainly fit the fundamental DD service philosophy of catalyzing and changing the service system as well as serving those children and adults unserved by the current system. It is a significant shift in the Council's role and the use of DD funds.

THE FORMULA GRANT

The previous sections in this chapter have all looked at what the state and the DD Council must and can do. In return, the federal government makes a cash allocation to each participating state.

A state's share of the total amount appropriated by Congress for the formula grant program is based on a three-part formula, hence the term *formula grant*. The 1972 regulations called for the following formula:

> Two-thirds of the grant is based on total population weighted by "financial needs" which is defined as "relative per capita income." The other third is calculated on need as "based on the scope and extent of services to be provided under the approved state plan."

The exact mathematics of the "formula" to include factors of "financial need" and need "based on the scope and extent of services to be provided" is too complicated to reproduce here. However, the financial need factor is figured by comparing the average national per capita income for the last 3 years for which the data are available with the average state per capita income for those 3 years. The other need factor is figured by comparing the number of beneficiaries in the state under the "Adult Disabled Child Program" of Social Security with the number of people in the state who are between the ages of 18 and 64. The data for these comparisons come from the Department of Commerce, the Social Security Administration, and the Census Bureau, and are updated periodically.

Originally, no state received less than $100,000 (except the territories of the Virgin Islands, Guam, American Samoa, and the Trust Territories of the Pacific). The 1975 law raised the minimum state allotment to $150,000 to all states, including the District of Columbia and Puerto Rico. The Virgin Islands, Guam, American Samoa, and Trust Territories of the Pacific received at least $50,000. The 1978 law has raised the minimum levels to $250,000 for states, the District of Columbia and Puerto Rico; the territories qualify for a $100,000 minimum.

CONCLUSION

There has always been an inherent tension in the identity of the developmental disabilities program. Is it a service provision program or a planning and influencing program? The two most significant changes made by the 1978 act continue this tension to some extent. The new broad, noncategorical definition of a developmental disability is well suited to a planning program. The four priority service provision areas tilt the program toward service provision despite the limited funds and expanded pool of eligible clients. The future role of DD Councils depends on the resolution of this tension.

REFERENCES

Federal Register, 1972, *37(176),* Part II. DD regulations for PL 91-517.
Federal Register, 1977, *42(18),* Part II. DD regulations for PL 94-103.
Mental Retardation Facilities and Community Health Center Construction Act of 1963. (As amended by Public Laws 90-1970, 91-517, 94-103, and 95-602.)

5

Two Faces of the Developmental Disabilities Movement

Ronald Wiegerink

The Developmentally Disabled Assistance and Bill of Rights Act of 1978 (PL 95-602) extended and amended the original 1970 legislation and the amendments of 1975. Signed into law October, 1978, by President Carter, this act provides the legal framework for what has become known as the developmental disabilities movement, an advocacy movement working to assure developmentally disabled citizens their human rights and services commensurate with their needs.

From the very beginning of the federal program there have been two faces to the developmental disabilities (DD) movement. On the optimistic side, the DD movement has been a leap forward in the right direction. On the cynical side, the movement, at best, has been a necessary diversion in a struggle for attaining services for handicapped persons.

Optimistic advocates see the developmental disabilities movement in the light of its goals: 1) to expand services for severely handicapped people; 2) to reduce duplication in services and resources; 3) to increase gap-filling services; 4) to marshal generic resources and services to aid developmentally disabled people; 5) to develop a consortium of state agency personnel, services providers, and consumers or consumer representatives in the comprehensive planning of services; and 7) to provide access for consumers to decision making that determines what they receive and when. These are necessary goals if the rights of developmentally disabled people and services designed to meet their needs are to be realized.

The cynics see the developmental disabilities movement as an inexpensive method of buying off advocates for handicapped and disabled people. The DD program gives each state and territory a small amount of money to conduct an overwhelming task. It establishes a foreign body, the Developmental Disabilities Council, in each state among existing state agencies. The Council is designed to coordinate disparate state and federal agencies and programs. Although the federal government cannot coordinate its own agencies' efforts, it directs a small body of people to attempt coordination at the state level. The DD program has been constantly subjected to changing and ambiguous regulations, guidelines, and requests. Consumer groups are sometimes reduced to fighting over small amounts of resources while millions of federal dollars go to other competing causes.

SOME PROBLEMS

Despite the recent passage of new supportive legislation, program conflicts remain at an impasse, and the DD movement is fighting for its integrity. Many state DD Councils have had to struggle for their very existence. Some have been disbanded again, primarily for political reasons. Is it possible that these Councils, made up of state agency heads, prominent professionals, service providers, and consumers, were engaged in such objectionable activities—on behalf of disabled people—that they needed to be publicly reprimanded and disbanded? Unlikely. More to the point, often they were establishing goals, defining objectives, and mobilizing resources to become potent forces on behalf of handicapped people. In a time of short monies and human resources, detractors inside of government with other goals and objectives consider DD mobilization to be threatening.

Some DD Councils have been immobilized in other ways. Councils have had to work with little staff or with staff whose loyalties lay elsewhere; most Councils have had to borrow their staff from the state administering agency. This has often led to conflicts of interests and divided loyalties for the assigned staff and has made interagency coordination a difficult, if not impossible, task. In some cases where there is a dedicated staff, too often manpower is inadequate to fulfill Council responsibilities. That is, time and skill for comprehensive planning, understanding of developmentally disabled people and their needs, and knowledge of essential political and legislative tasks are in short supply.

Because DD Councils have often had difficulty in developing their organizational goals, structures, and resources, they have spent their time acting as mini-agencies, passing out service grants from minuscule formula grant funds. As a result, the major responsibilities of comprehensive planning, carefully selected gap-filling activities, provision of access to resources, program development, and policy monitoring have been often neglected. Service grant-giving activities have led to squabbles among Council members and conflicts with state agencies, which have a responsibility to inspect service delivery systems. These conflicts have been counterproductive to DD Councils' goals of coordination and cooperation.

In other instances, DD Councils have been co-opted by their administering agencies. Various strategies have been used, but the result is usually the same: the administering agency prepares the State Plan, sets the priorities, divides the monies into administrative support services and service grants, and, in the eleventh hour, seeks the rubber stamp approval of the DD Councils. Councils in this position do not meet often enough to organize resistance to this type of approach. Too often, this modus operandi results in stagnation and apathy; the Council fails to exercise any advocacy function adequately, let alone its legitimate planning function.

SOME PROGRESS

Lest this appear too negative, let me point out that ineffective Councils have continued to dwindle in number. In most states, Councils have solved their problems and have shifted their focus to planning, advising, monitoring, and advocating. In 21 states, statutory legislation has established the Council and its functions as a permanent body of state government. Thirty states have had executive orders to support the Council's role in planning and advocating (Brunninghaus and Wiegerink, 1976). There has been a steady trend toward enhancing visibility of DD Councils in state government (EMC, 1978). Advisory Councils once assigned to low-level divisions within agencies (e.g., the Division of Mental Retardation within the Department of Mental Health) have now become Planning Councils attached to high-level Human Resource Departments, or to the Governor's Planning Offices. This upward trend acknowledges and stabilizes the Councils' meaningful role and the importance of the consumers they are attempting to serve.

Councils are taking direct action in reviewing state legislation and standards as they affect the rights of handicapped people. Some have proposed and monitored legislation and standards, while others have exposed rights guaranteed but not observed, by law. Over 40 Councils have established monetary, evaluative, and legislative committees and task forces, some employing legal staff, to assist in these activities. Some, with the support of the National Center for Law and the Handicapped at South Bend, Indiana, have acted as "friends of the court" in legal action.

DD Councils have accessed other federal legislation in order to gain resources for developmentally disabled people. Most councils have targeted the Supplemental Security Income program and Revenue Sharing as sources of direct support and services for disabled citizens. DD Councils have also influenced Title XX social service plans, assuring inclusion of disabled people. Other resources, such as the Housing and Development Act and the Comprehensive Employment and Training Act (CETA), have proved useful in providing resources for developmentally disabled persons. In these efforts, DD resources have been used as seed monies to produce multiple effects.

Perhaps one of the most common activities of the DD program is the emphasis on public awareness. Almost half of the DD Councils across the country have established public awareness as one of their top priorities. They have produced and made available public information programs through radio, television, and newspapers for a variety of targeted audiences. They have held public hearings and forums. They have established hot lines and public information centers. Along with the public awareness efforts of consumer organizations, DD Councils are rapidly introducing the general public to the needs of developmentally disabled people and the resources available for them.

A growing number of Councils see their role of monitor and advocate as one of primary importance. Three-fourths of the Councils have systems advisory committees (EMC, 1978). These committees review major service programs, develop standards and regulations, review seed grants and granting procedures, and make on-site visits to residential programs. Often, the outcome of these activities is to motivate the Council to advocate for new legislation, new monies, and new forms of coordination and cooperation among agencies and service providers.

To assist in these efforts and others, over one-half of the Councils have established regional mechanisms within their states (Brunninghaus and Wiegerink, 1976). These mechanisms range from regional hearings, to committees, to regional Councils with paid staff budgets. The regional mechanisms have been used to assess needs, develop regional plans, give service grants, monitor services, and conduct public awareness activities. It appears that these mechanisms are very useful and cost-effective and are much needed to give the DD Councils statewide impact.

All Councils have helped to develop gap-filling, innovative services for their states. For example, the North Carolina DD Council has assisted in developing a network of 12 group homes under the auspices of the Methodist Church; Florida has developed a statewide system for assessing the medication needs of epileptic citizens in its state; Rhode Island has developed an interagency early education screening, diagnostic, and treatment program; Kentucky has developed a hortotherapy program, providing work for handicapped persons in a network of private or profit green houses; and Tennessee has developed a coordination system for one of its service delivery regions that assures interagency communication and identifies gaps in services. In most cases, these and other states have used some of their formula grant monies to pay for direct service projects to fill existing gaps and to develop programs that would eventually be funded by other sources. This seed money approach has been one of the most common and successful methods for developing the role and credibility of DD Councils, while at the same time setting the stage for their involvement in policy issues and decisions.

CONCLUSION

Fortunately, the developmental disabilities program got another boost with the passage and signing of the Developmentally Disabled Assistance and Bill of Rights Act of 1978. The act:

1. Expands the definition of developmental disabilities to become more cross categorical
2. Increases consumer memberships on the Councils to at least one-half of the membership
3. Increases the formula grant program
4. Focuses planning on three service areas: childhood, nonvocational training of adults, and community alternatives
5. Reaffirms an emphasis on deinstitutionalization
6. Expands the Protection and Advocacy Program
7. Calls for a national evaluation system to be in place by 1982

These are only a few of the notable features of the legislation.

Most important, because of the new legislation the developmental disabilities movement continues to prosper. However, the program is now larger than legislation itself. It is a movement of advocates who work with passion and competence to improve the quality of life for handicapped citizens. From any perspective, the DD movement is facing in the right direction.

REFERENCES

Bruninghaus, R., and Wiegerink, R. *Profiles of DD Councils*. Chapel Hill, N.C.: DDTAS, 1976.

Program Issue Review, *The Characteristics of Developmental Disabilities State Planning Councils*. Philadelphia: EMC Institute, 1978.

Part II
ADVOCACY

Advocacy is one of the most important elements in the conceptual framework underlying the DD movement. Part II includes four chapters that describe different forms advocacy can take. Together, they provide a comprehensive view of advocacy and the issues and problems to be considered.

They also provide the primary components for a "system" of advocacy. Many of the activities discussed in these chapters are already ongoing in most states. What has not occurred in most states is a purposeful linking between certain advocacy programs that should be linked. These linkages would foster the development of an advocacy system. These chapters should be useful to those concerned with building more comprehensive models of advocacy.

Ronald Neufeld's "The Advocacy Role and Function of Developmental Disabilities Councils" is informative about the antecedents of the advocacy concept. He describes the relatively recent rekindling of interest in advocacy and discusses some of the reasons for it. He contrasts two forms of advocacy, internal and external, pointing out both positive and negative aspects associated

with each approach. He then elaborates on the importance of the advocacy role to DD Councils, suggesting a variety of advocacy-oriented activities in which they can engage.

In "Examining Consumers' Assumptions," H. Rutherford and Ann P. Turnbull address the matter of advocacy not only as professionals involved with both the legal rights of handicapped persons and special education but as the parents of a moderately retarded child as well. The Rutherfords identify and probe many of the assumptions held by advocates and explain how effective advocacy must stem from these assumptions.

Donald O. Mayer, in "Legal Advocacy for Developmentally Disabled People," identifies the responsibilities and functions of the legal advocate at four distinct levels: institutional, community, state-wide, and national. Mayer explains the individual role of each level and proposes ways for each to effectively interact with the others.

The last chapter in this part, "Self-Advocacy and Changing Attitudes" by Rita A. Varela, provides yet another dimension to advocacy activity.

Ms. Varela's chapter introduces the need for alternative approaches by pointing out several problems arising out of the relationship between people who have disabilities and those who provide services to them. She then examines three major themes underlying the self-advocacy movement and concludes with a statement about the potential positive effect of increased self-advocacy on the service delivery system.

6

The Advocacy Role
and Functions of
Developmental Disabilities Councils

G. Ronald Neufeld

The recent conceptual evolution of advocacy has been thwarted by confusing definitions. Advocacy was popularized several years ago when federal funds were released to launch a number of experimental advocacy programs. Since then a large number of programs and projects bearing an advocacy label have appeared. A close examination of those activities labeled as advocacy would fail to produce a unique theme that would distinguish them from many other human service enterprises. The question then must be raised: What is unique about advocacy?

To begin with, advocacy broadly considered is a set of beliefs that result in action aimed at defending, maintaining, or promoting a cause. Advocacy activity interacts both with individuals and with the systems that have been created to serve individuals. From an individual perspective, advocacy involves acting in behalf of, or pleading a cause for, another. It may take the form of an able person fighting for someone who is not able to fight for himself, maintain his cause, or protect his own human rights. The uniqueness of an advocacy perspective is perhaps most clearly visible at the point where advocacy interacts with the systems that exist to serve handicapped clients. It is the advocate's belief that a program should be accountable to the clients it serves. The effectiveness of a system should be measured by its responsiveness to client needs in contrast to system maintenance needs or the convenience of a system's staff. An advocacy perspective starts with the client and attempts to examine services through the eyes of the client. The orientation of the advocacy approach to the human rights of the individual client is so strong that the advocate's style might be characterized as zealous. An advocate is fanatically devoted and partisan to his client. If need be, an advocate is willing to fight for a cause in behalf of his client despite resistance and intimidation from the system.

Advocacy as an individual activity is as old as the human race. In fact, a very important dimension of child rearing is directed toward training a child to be an advocate for himself. For an individual to successfully enter adulthood implies that he has attained a relatively high level of independence. That means, in part, that he has become a self-advocate. One aspect of normalization training for handicapped persons involves helping them to reach their highest possible level of independence or to increase their ability to advocate for themselves.

Beyond an individual, the family in our social structure is viewed as the basic advocacy unit. The family bears responsibility to its dependent young and handicapped members to engage in advocacy activities. In rural America, the family, the church, or the community was often highly successful in advocating for the needs of their respective memberships. It was often true that rural families lacked access to caregiving facilities for handicapped persons outside of their own communities.

In a small community, handicapped persons were probably known by all of the residents. The strengths and limitations of persons were likely to be known by everyone, and in many instances, community support was generated for the handicapped person and the family. Emotional support was available for the family, and corporate care was provided for the person as care was needed, ranging from personal supervision to the supervision of work that the handicapped person could manage.

Along with the industrialization and urbanization of our social structure, we have witnessed a breakdown in family and community solidarity. With this breakdown, the capability of families, churches, and communities to advocate for their members has diminished. Given the size, complexity, and impersonal nature of many of our human service arrangements, it is often impossible for even competent and highly independent individuals to advocate for themselves. Despite competence levels, individuals are often ruthlessly dominated by large organizations.

Due to the apparent breakdown of the informal, human advocacy procedures that have operated in the past, we are confronted by a need to identify some new advocacy approaches. In this chapter, the clients needing advocacy are the developmentally disabled, a minority population whose cries are seldom heard in the political and bureaucratic streams of local, state, and federal organizations. Unlike the informal, unstructured advocacy techniques of the past, the time has come to consider the value of promoting the concept of advocacy for the developmentally disabled as a social movement. What is needed is a movement aimed at assuring the human rights of the developmentally disabled person; a movement aimed at rendering services that are accountable to clients; a movement committed to identifying and providing support for effective advocates; and a movement geared toward a functional yoking together of individual advocates.

In order for advocacy for developmentally disabled persons to flourish as a social movement, several alliances are need. Those alliances include developmentally disabled consumers; nonhandicapped advocates for developmentally disabled persons; professionals and nonprofessionals; programs in institutions and communities; a variety of fragmented categorical groupings; and, finally, representatives from the public and private sector. The intention in this chapter is to explore the potential of Developmental Disabilities Councils to function as advocacy mechanisms within the system. It focuses primarily upon the merger that is needed between the public and the private sector, or the alliance between advocates inside the system and advocates outside the system.

INTERNAL AND EXTERNAL ADVOCACY ACTIVITY

Two forms of advocacy activity have emerged so far. They can be characterized as internal and external advocacy. Internal advocates work within the systems that support them, whereas external advocates receive support from sources that are independent from the systems in which they perform their advocacy activities. One major objection to internal advocacy programs is that advocates in the system lose too much freedom to act in an objective, unbiased fashion in behalf of their clients. "Whose bread I eat, his song I sing." To the extent that this adage is true, advocating within the system is a disadvantage. When client advocacy activity results in conflict between the advocate and the system providing his support, an advocate may feel pressured to compromise an ideal. It is difficult to bite a feeding hand. If a system resists the advocacy activity of the advocates it sponsors, it may employ a variety of "cooling out" tactics. For example, advocates may receive work assignments that create distance between advocates and their clients. The risks of system co-option or "cooling out" suggest that there may be an advantage to providing independent support for the work of advocacy to give assurance that the system in which the advocates work will not control them.

One of the advantages of advocacy from within the system is that advocates are likely to have greater access to information about programs serving their clients. External advocates tend to be adversaries of the system. System adversaries are often disliked by service providers and they are therefore denied access to the service delivery settings and to important sources of information. If advocates cannot monitor the delivery system directly, then the information on which they base their actions must be second-hand information. The actions and accusations of advocates must be based on accurate information. A rapid erosion of advocacy credibility will result from actions and accusations based upon false information or incomplete data. System adversaries may be viewed as Quixotes tilting with windmills. They do not know the issues and they do not know the enemies.

Another important difference between internal and external advocacy concerns the tactics they employ. Internal advocates are likely to believe that human service systems can be renewed and that this renewal can be accomplished from within the system. When they are faced with a problem, their first approach is to bring about change by negotiation. Confrontation is a last resort.

It has already been pointed out that external advocates are often characterized by a strong negative system bias. They contend that our current human service systems are beyond redemption and must be dismantled. Their intent is to destroy and start anew. They view negotiation with the human service establishment as a waste of time and move immediately to confrontation. Caught up as they often are with their obsession to tear down the existing structures of the system, they sometimes overlook their advocacy goals and fail to foresee the injuries that their clients may suffer in the system dismantling process. In addition, the external advocate may not be able to offer the support a client may need if existing services are withdrawn. They may see the problems, but stop short of providing solutions, much like the terrier chasing a locomotive. What will he do with it when he catches it? There are many natural advocates and potential advocacy allies in the system. A wholesale condemnation of the system, of all of its parts and all of its personnel, is likely to stand in the way of an alliance between the internal resources and an advocacy movement.

Another disadvantage of external advocacy programs is that they tend to be transient. Financial support is often small and short-term. A single charismatic leader is often responsible for the genesis and direction of the program. Generally, a small band of highly committed persons work toward solving a small number of specific problems. When the problems are solved or appear insoluble, when financial support collapses or when the leader disappears, the movement is likely to vanish.

The foregoing polarization of internal and external advocacy activity is seldom witnessed in the extreme forms described. However the distinction between internal and external advocacy is a useful one in order to help Council advocates consider the strengths and weaknesses of the different approaches. Despite the differences between the internal and external advocacy approaches it is likely that they would agree upon the problems facing developmentally disabled persons. The differences between the two approaches concern the tactics they use. Obviously there are advantages and disadvantages to both internal and external advocacy approaches. For advocacy to become an effective social movement, it will be necessary to integrate the strengths from both approaches. This entails the development of an advocacy mechanism within the system that has a strong alliance with organization from the private sector.

It is intended in this chapter to examine the capability of DD Councils to function as advocacy structures within the system at the level of state government. The role and functions of Councils as outlined by federal legislation (PL 91-517) include a number of provisions that enable them to undertake advocacy responsibility for developmentally disabled persons. Among the legislative provisions that establish internal advocacy functions are comprehensive planning for developmentally disabled persons, service coordination, and service monitoring. In order to plan, coordinate, and monitor, governor-appointed state councils have been established. These councils include membership from several consumer groups and a variety of state agencies. An attempt is made in the following discussion to indicate the kind of advocacy activity that DD Councils can provide for developmentally disabled clients at the level of state government.

ACCOUNTABILITY AND MONITORING

As internal advocates for developmentally disabled persons, one of the functions of a DD Council is to render the human services network, from the level of state agencies to the level of the service delivery network, appropriately accountable to developmentally disabled persons. Over time, human service programs often seem to be guilty of misdirecting accountability. That is to say, many public programs are self-serving and more responsive to the needs of their employees than they are to the public and their clients. In a democracy, the principle is generally accepted that the elected government and its administration must be accountable to the people. Accountability is a strong word. At the very lowest level it embraces the notion of a tie, an allegiance, or a commitment. At another level, accountability means answerable to, responsible to, and dependent upon. If state programs are answerable to and dependent upon the public, exposure to the public and openness is implied. In many instances, decisions in human service systems are made with the convenience of the staff in mind rather than the needs of the clients. Employees often find themselves answering primarily to other employees or working to maintain the system for staff convenience. Client needs become secondary. Staff-centered programs are likely to be closed systems in the sense that they resist external investigations and are not open to the public. Exposure to the public might result in criticism or a loss of the privileges and advantages that staff-centered programs provide.

When an employee in a public service program must make a decision between self-serving action or action in behalf of the clients, it is clear that the client should be served. Occasionally, however, public employees are confronted with making decisions between conflicting interests. In such an instance, a "right" decision may be more difficult to find. A "decide for yourself example" is presented below. Let us suppose it has been reported to an elected state official that state cars are being used for private purposes. One solution that has been proposed to prevent this abuse is that decals be placed on all state cars. Cars from a residential school for emotionally disturbed youth are identified with a state psychiatric hospital. On several occasions the students are embarrassed when riding in the marked state cars, and they are harassed by local youth because of the association with a psychiatric facility. In this instance the state official is faced with conflicting accountability. On the one hand, the official may feel a need to protect the interests of the general public, who elected him, against the misuse of state property. On the other hand, the state official should feel a keen sense of responsibility for the accountability to the emotionally disturbed population entrusted to his care. The psychological and emotional welfare of the residents in the state school should prevail over the financial considerations of the political constituents. However, in situations such as the one presented, the public official may choose to support a decision that is not in the best interest of the minority disenfranchised population. When this is the case, advocates are needed to help protect the rights and interests of the handicapped persons.

A variety of advocacy mechanisms is needed to assure appropriately directed accountability. Self-serving bureaucracies need to be confronted and state officials need support for making responsible decisions in favor of developmentally disabled clients (consumers). Aggressive support for state officials is especially necessary when decisions in favor of a minority group may result in a loss of political support from the general public. Developmental Disabilities Councils are in a position to provide support for advocates in the system. Councils also have the potential to assure properly directed accountability in the human service delivery system.

Next, several techniques are presented that a Council can employ to assure accountability to developmentally disabled clients.

One technique a Council can use to assure properly directed service accountability is to monitor human service programs. One of the advantages of monitoring programs is that services often improve simply as a function of monitoring. Several investigations provide support for this observation. For example, Dr. O. Lindsley, who developed the precision teaching procedure, once attempted to identify a variety of factors that contributed to change in human behavior (1972). None of the interventions investigated appeared to make a difference. The single significant variable that appeared to affect behavioral change was the process of data collection itself. In an experiment conducted by Dr. J. Reid (undated), it was discovered that the accuracy of data collected by behavior observers increased when they were being watched. Similarly, in their experiments with oppositional children, Dr. G. Patterson and Alice Harris (undated) discovered that interaction within family units changed when observers were present.

The point is that in many instances it has been demonstrated that the behavior changes if subjects know they are being watched or monitored. With this in mind, perhaps improved or redirected program accountability could be accomplished if a variety of monitoring procedures was established to watch service providers. Perhaps developmentally disabled persons would be guaranteed their fair share of public resources if the decisions of elected officials and the activity of state agencies were monitored by mechanisms advocating for the developmentally disabled. At the service delivery level, perhaps monitoring service providers would result in more responsive programs for developmentally disabled persons. At the individual level, it is likely that monitoring would assure more effective use of existing services and provide information concerning the need for new programs.

There is no shortcut to individual client monitoring. Although the most effective watching is provided by the members of a client's family, there are times when the family may not be fully aware of a client's needs or of the services that are available. For this reason the parents of handicapped persons should be trained to recognize client needs and be apprised of the resources that can meet those needs. In some instances, client monitoring within the family may not be sufficient. In the absence of support by trained professionals, some communities have successfully organized groups of volunteers that can function as extensions of the family. Once again, volunteers cannot be expected to function successfully without substantial training concerning client needs and available and needed resources. Hence, professionals trained to recognize areas of unmet client needs to identify and access available resources must launch extensive recruitment and training programs aimed at mobilizing neighborhood and community-based organizations.

At another level, the quality of service provision for developmentally disabled clients should be checked by program monitoring. Programs should be checked to guarantee that the rights and interests of clients are protected, that the service provided is responsive to client needs, and that the physical facilities are designed in the best interest of the client. Substantial knowledge about human service programs is required at this level of monitoring. On one hand, program monitors must know how to identify program weaknesses. At the same time, they should be aware of program alternatives for service delivery. In this way an advocate as a monitor can offer constructive criticism when program weaknesses are exposed and can negotiate change.

Despite industry's recognition of the need for quality control, monitoring has never been viewed as a necessary procedure for quality control in human service settings. Traditionally, the general public has invested blind trust in professionals and service providers to "do good" and has refused to get involved. To suggest the need for monitoring in the human service delivery system smacks of distrust. Service providers tend to recoil with defensiveness, suspicion, and counter-proposals to "cool-out" the monitors. Yet the recent exposés of human abuses in institutional settings, such as Willowbrook in New York and Parsons State Hospital in Alabama, clearly indicate the need for program monitoring in residential settings. The periodic program reviews or site visits often sponsored by the state departments responsible for these programs are seldom adequate monitoring procedures. It is too easy for program staff to hide program weaknesses behind brief, superficial investigations. The occasional inquisition of a dedicated newsman or a consumer organization will also often result in employee routs and reorganization. However, the renewal resulting from this kind of monitoring is often short lived.

A few institutions, recognizing the need for constant program monitoring, have been attracted to the concept of advocacy as a way to monitor their programs and assure service accountability to their clients. In one such institution, a team of five advocates has been hired to monitor services provided for 700 residents. They are accountable directly to the superintendent. When they encounter violations of resident rights or program weaknesses, the advocates set in motion a process of negotiation with the staff to correct the problems. If there is disagreement between the staff member and the advocate, or if the staff person fails to make program changes in the interest of the client, confrontation is used. Unresolved conflicts are taken directly to the superintendent and the Human Rights Committee. The Human Rights Committee consists of institution staff, residents, and the parents of residents.

Advocacy designs like the one described may have value not only for program monitoring but also for tracking clients on an individual basis to assure the appropriate provision of services. Program weaknesses are often exposed by this monitoring procedure. The problems of this design are the same disadvantages specified for all internal advocacy activity. The risk is co-option or "cooling out." Furthermore, if the hiring of advocates is a decision that institution administrators are free to make, then institutions that most require monitoring services are likely to be the ones that will resist advocacy services. Ideally, advocacy in institutions should be externally accountable, and advocates should be paid from an outside source. One suggestion is that DD Councils establish local or regional councils to whom advocates would report. Finally, advocates as monitors must develop excellent data collection skills. It has already been pointed out that nothing can erode the credibility of advocacy activity with greater speed than false information.

Another technique for program monitoring that is currently in use is the application of program standards for community and regional institutions. Apart from standards developed by individual states for their own use, the standards for residential facilities and standards for community agencies developed by the Joint Commission on Accreditation of Hospitals are the most widely known and used. These standards are particularly useful for indicating program gaps and weaknesses.

The ombudsman model developed in the Scandinavian countries is another monitoring procedure for programs at the state level. Effective advocacy by ombudsmen requires the direct flow of information from clients to the ombudsman. When the ombudsman is confronted with unmet client needs or violations of client rights, an attempt is made to eliminate the cause of the unmet need or rights violation at the system level. Successful ombudsman activity calls for a substantial power base inside the system.

The need for client and program monitoring was recognized by the staff of Child Advocacy System Project, a neighborhood advocacy program conducted in Morganton, North Carolina. Two procedures were developed in this project, one, a procedure for monitoring individual clients (Pelosi and Johnson, 1974), and, two, a procedure for monitoring programs (Holder, Pelosi, and Dixon, 1974). The individual monitoring procedure suggests a procedure for helping monitors to recognize when advocacy is of the client. The program monitoring procedure suggests approaches to identify program weaknesses from a client perspective, and suggests ways to render programs accountable to their clients.

An important consideration in service monitoring is the location in state government of the monitoring mechanism. Effective monitoring is unlikely to be effective outside of the agency in which the monitor is lodged. Unless the monitoring mechanism has substantial support from outside of the system, then it must depend entirely upon support from the chief executive in the host agency. The best insurance for effective monitoring is a network of councils extending from neighborhoods, to counties, to multicounty districts. These councils should involve citizens and have substantial support from the private sector. At present, the councils can look toward consumer or parent groups, such as the associations for retarded children or some of the emerging non-categorical consumer organizations.

Despite the negative reception that the concept of monitoring is likely to encounter in human service settings, service monitoring is an important aspect of assuring programs that are accountable to developmentally disabled clients. Monitoring should take place at all levels of activity, ranging from the client, to the service delivery system, to the state agency. Monitoring sponsored by a system needs the unqualified support of the chief executive in the program or agency in which it is located, and monitoring outside of that agency is likely to be ineffective. The chances for effective monitoring are increased when the monitoring agency has support from the private sector. Finally, the results of monitoring need to be communicated to persons or organizations that can bring about change in those systems.

COMMUNICATION

The story is told of a farmer in Maine who had a telephone installed in his home. One night, while a neighbor was visiting the farmer, his phone began to ring. Despite repeated calls, the farmer refused to answer his telephone. When asked why he failed to pick up his receiver, the farmer replied, "I had that durn thing installed for my convenience."

The human service delivery system cannot afford the luxury of one-way communication. Communication concerning citizen needs and problems must flow from communities to state program administrators. Some organization must then assume responsibility for apprising the public and legislators concerning the needs of developmentally disabled persons. Finally, the communication cycle is not complete until the public is apprised of the various programs and interventions that are created in response to client needs.

Since communication exchange concerning human service delivery is weak in most states, DD Councils might assume responsibility for establishing a comprehensive communication network.

At the level of state programs, communication between state agencies is essential if the Council is to accomplish the work of comprehensive planning and service coordination and if it is to influence human services from an advocacy perspective. Change that can be accomplished through negotiation is likely to be more effective than change that is sought as a consequence of confrontation. Although all of the changes that may be needed to support the rights and interests of the developmentally disabled person may not be accomplished through negotiation, negotiation should be the first tactic employed. Confrontation should be a last resort. Negotiation requires communication. For this reason, Councils must set up a system of internal communication with all parts of the human service network at the state level that it hopes to influence.

Councils, as advocacy mechanisms, must also develop a system of information exchange between the public and the private sector. It is often true that state agencies and human service programs become closed systems because they try to hide program weaknesses. Inevitably program weaknesses that threaten program administrators are exposed to the public. In the wake of inquisitions and public exposés, employees are often fired and programs reorganized. Inquisitions and public exposés do not guarantee constructive changes. However, the public has a right to information concerning both the strengths and weaknesses of the programs that are supported by public funds. Given this knowledge, the public has responsibility for identifying and helping to provide solutions to the problems that face its programs. It seems that this kind of openness with the public would tend to reduce the number of program investigations that result in shocking disclosures and public recoil. An appropriate function of Councils is to create a channel of communication between public programs and the public. Support from the private sector cannot be expected unless this kind of communication exists.

One strategy that a Council might use to provide information to the public concerning the delivery of services to developmentally disabled clients is to hire a communication specialist to communicate with the public through radio, television, and the press. This person should be familiar with all programs serving developmentally disabled clients in his area, and he should know how to collect information concerning interactions between the dispensers and receivers of care. The communication specialist would agree to spend a proportion of his time collecting data in human service programs. This data could then be reported to citizens in the community through newspaper articles, by news releases to television and radio stations, and by public presentations to civic organizations and groups, such as school boards or local parent and teacher associations. Citizens might be left to judge the nature of the interactions, but both negative and positive incidents should be reported.

It is interesting to speculate on the potential power of such a communication design to render the service delivery system more responsive to the public and its clients. It is hoped that the public would become more knowledgeable concerning its programs, and subsequently would become more involved. Perhaps Council action groups would organize to improve weak programs and support would be generated for the natural advocates that would be identified.

In order to initiate communication between state organizations and local citizens, the DD Council in Utah conducted a series of televised public hearings. The hearings were held in seven different locations in the state. Persons were contacted in each county to disseminate information concerning the hearings and to make local arrangements. Letters announcing the meetings were sent to parents of handicapped persons, agencies working with the handicapped, state legislators, educators, and local and county officials. An attempt was made to avoid holding the meetings in facilities that were associated with a particular agency or program.

Six to eight members of the State Council conducted the hearings. All local citizens coming to the meeting were enrolled at the door and asked if they wished to speak. If so, they were invited to speak in the order in which they enrolled. Because speeches were often spontaneous, tape recordings were made and stenographic notes were taken. Citizens who did not wish to speak were invited to submit written statements. After the citizens had spoken, raised issues, or asked questions, members of the council, agency personnel, or legislators responded. Citizens attending the meetings ranged in number from 15 to 400.

The recurring theme expressed at the hearings was the need for increased money in special education; removal of the categories of mental retardation, learning disabilities, and emotional disturbance; community training programs for the adult handicapped, especially the severely disabled not eligible for rehabilitation services; recreation and transportation; early diagnosis and intervention; parent training; community-based residential alternatives in addition to state institutions; elimination of architectural barriers; and access to information about services. It seems likely that knowledgeable professionals would have identified a similar list of needs. This kind of information should generate greater confidence among professionals in developing closer ties with citizens from the private sector.

The citizens who participated in the Utah hearings indicated that they were pleased to have a forum in which they could express their concerns, frustration, and anger. They expressed a desire for more hearings in other parts of the state, especially in rural areas. During the hearings, parents of developmentally disabled persons were made aware of services in their area that they had not known of previously.

In addition to learning of needs from citizens, there were numerous advantages in the hearings to the Council itself. First, the Council's visibility was increased and its identity established, and second, the hearings resulted in improved communication between citizens and the Council.

In addition to the television coverage of the hearings, news releases were sent to local weekly newspapers, and hearings in the more populous areas of the state were covered by daily newspapers with statewide circulation. The example cited contains many ingredients of a sound communication system. It included face-to-face encounter between citizens and state-level program administrators. It encouraged private citizens to make statements concerning needs as they saw them, and it gave the public an opportunity to ask questions of state employees. The information emanating from the hearings was disseminated, using television and the press. This would seem to be a good starting point for a sound and comprehensive communication network between state programs and local citizens. It could also provide initiative for the private sector to organize into action groups.

There are, of course, many ways in which communication exchange can be accomplished in a state. In some states, films, slide-tape presentations, and pamphlets or fliers are produced in order to disseminate information concerning client needs and services. Conferences and workshops are also conducted to bring together various interest groups and develop action plans.

In this writer's opinion, all of these activities are needed to assure complete information sharing among legislators, state agencies, consumer organizations, local government agencies, service delivery units, and private citizens. The sharing of this information should not be left to chance. Rather, a careful design accounting for all parts of the social structure should be developed. At every level careful consideration should be given to the communication technique that is most effective.

THE PUBLIC ALLIANCE

It has already been pointed out that an effective advocacy system requires an alliance between the public and private sectors. Staff that are supported by developmental disabilities resources usually receive their salaries from a state agency. In this sense they are part of the state system and run the risk of becoming an additional agency of state government and being "cooled out" like any other internal advocacy mechanism. Unlike most state agencies, DD Councils have the opportunity of relating to a council that consists of a variety of state agencies and several consumer agencies. Persons supported by developmental disability funds might be viewed as advocates within the system. The external advocates are private citizens working for and committed to the developmental disabilities movement. Staff to the Councils should be viewed as seams in the fabric that bring together not only the public and the private sector but also the professionals or service providers and the nonprofessional citizen.

Historically, many parents of handicapped children have abdicated program responsibility and service delivery to professionals. Unfortunately, professionals alone have been unable to develop a system of services that adequately responds to the needs of handicapped persons in this country. On one hand, there are tremendous gaps between services, and many handicapped persons are not provided with the help and support they need. On the other hand, there are many overlapping services and scarce resources are wasted. Finally, many of the services that exist are inflexible and unresponsive despite information that indicates the need for change.

In some instances, professionals point out that the parents prefer to be relieved of responsibility for handicapped persons. Additionally, the general public tends to have a narrow range of tolerance for physical or behavioral variance. Professionals point out that even if public citizens wish to become involved in service delivery as volunteers, training them takes more time than it is worth. To the extent that these attitudes exist, one can understand the impulse of professionals to undertake program development and service delivery without involving parents or the general public.

If professionals were adequately serving the needs of handicapped persons without help from parents and other public citizens, we could accept their independence. However, since confusion seems to reign in the human service network and since we continue to be faced with many unmet needs, a strong case can be made for the development of sound linkages with the general public.

Areas of support that can be provided by the general public range from direct service and individual and program monitoring to participation on boards and political lobbying. In each of these areas, professionals should assume responsibility for recruitment, organization, and training.

In the area of direct service, it is clear that in the foreseeable future there will not be sufficient public resources to provide the kind of staff-to-client ratios that are necessary to adequately serve the needs of developmentally disabled persons. At the same time, the interest of parents and their potential for providing service has not been realized.

The Regional Intervention Program in Nashville, Tennessee, provides us with an example of an excellent, cost-effective program for emotionally handicapped children utilizing citizen participation. Parents applying to have their children admitted for treatment must agree to receive training and work in the programs for 6 months after their child has graduated. In this way, the project functions with only two full-time staff members and backup consultation from professionals.

In Nebraska, a program of "live-in friend" involves a citizen advocate sharing an apartment with a retarded person who has been discharged from a residential institution. The occupations of "live-in friends" have included students, social workers, teachers, salesmen, and secretaries. In most instances the "live-in friends" are not paid for their participation in the program. The "live-in friends" are benefactors (Heber and Dever, 1970) and teachers for their roommate in money management, shopping, use of public transportation, cooking, self-medication, use of telephones, and leisure time activities. It has been reported that the program is effective and economical (Perske and Marquiss, 1973).

The concept of "benefactor," which undergirds the "live-in friend," originated from a study of persons discharged from a residential institution in California and who made successful adjustments to the cultural mainstream. In his research, Edgerton (1967) reports that the critical factor in community adjustment was the relationship of a retarded person to a benefactor. Benefactors helped them maintain: "(a) their self respect; (b) their ability to cope with the world; and (c) their ability to 'pass' for normal and to deny their mental retardation."

The foregoing examples of citizen participation in direct service activity are presented to indicate the need to capture a large potential source of manpower. It is likely that there are many persons employed in private enterprises with a keen sense of altruism and no outlet for that impulse.

In addition to direct service activity, there are other areas of activity in which support is needed from the private sector. For example, action that is highly controversial should in most instances be undertaken by groups or persons from the private sector. Confrontation by staff members of the Council may result in a breakdown of communication in the system or may absorb so much staff time that the work of planning and coordination may be ignored.

At other times effective employees in state programs or working for the Councils may sometimes need protection from fickle political machinery. Human services need to be depoliticized. In the meantime, protection from the political system is most effective when it emanates from the private sector. Support is also needed from the private sector in the area of lobbying and legislation. In the past, consumer organizations, such as associations for retarded children, have been most successful in obtaining the passage of legislation favoring developmentally disabled persons. While professionals can help in the work of organization and training, it is the weight of consumers that will produce political action.

Finally, it is becoming increasingly popular to establish boards with consumer representation. To the extent that this trend continues, Councils for the developmentally disabled need to recognize the need to provide training and education that enables consumers to function in more than token roles on boards.

CONCLUSION

Successful direct service activity is difficult to provide from the state level. One reason is that the state is too far removed from the service delivery setting to be adequately sensitive to the client needs. Among the products of state-operated programs are the large regional institutions that exist across the country. In order to operate these institutions and in order to manage other aspects of service delivery from the state, top-heavy administrative organizations tend to develop. In many instances planners, personnel departments, and fiscal agents are not adequately in touch with consumers to know their needs. In order to exercise control from a distance, state agencies tend to develop rules, regulations, and reporting procedures that seriously hamper program staff. In addition, a large regional institution has its own impersonal routines to regulate the daily movement of staff and residents. The result is often a "top-heavy," client-insensitive system that spends the bulk of its energy and resources maintaining itself.

One alternative is to keep services small and numerous, in order that the services be located close to the consumers, thus enabling consumers to remain close to their natural environments. These services might then be made accountable to local boards. If the model of locally operated programs were adopted, the role of state agencies would shift from service provision to enabling and monitoring. State agencies would focus upon planning, resource acquisition, training, information dissemination, organizational work, and monitoring.

To the extent that state agencies should be cautious concerning their involvement with direct service provision, this is even more true for Developmental Disabilities Councils. Persons and organizations with an advocacy perspective are often easily seduced into case advocacy activity. At this point it seems prudent to advise Councils to assume the role of *enabler* rather than the role of *doer* of advocacy activity. Since state agencies have the resources for service provision, the business of direct service should be left to them. The Council might work toward creating the kind of regional and local organizations that would eventually lead to decentralization and local service delivery, unifying all components of the system and bringing about an alliance between the public and the private sector. Service coordination is likely to be accomplished with greater ease at the local than at the state level.

If Councils attempt to provide direct service to clients, they will find that their meager resources will soon be gone and they will have little to show in terms of ongoing activity. In addition, the time required to engage the action needed for case advocacy would soon absorb all of the time of staff and Council alike, and no time would be left for planning, coordinating, and communicating. Advocacy as direct service activity inevitably results in high profile controversial activity. Given the recency of developmental disabilities legislation and the recency of Council interaction with programs at the state level, high profile, controversial activity may result in a premature death of the Councils and the developmental disabilities movement. Council staff should spend their time in administrative-enabling activity. As advocates inside the system, they should work toward developing an alliance with the private sector, the external advocates, and help them develop their skills in accountability procedures and service provision.

REFERENCES

Edgerton, R.B. *The Cloak of Competence: Stigma in the Lives of the Retarded.* Berkeley, Cal.: University of California Press, 1967.

Heber, R.F., and Dever, R.B. Research on education and habilitation of the mentally retarded. In H.C. Haywood (Ed.), *Social-Cultural Aspects of Mental Retardation.* New York: Appleton-Century-Crofts, 1970.

Holder, H.D., Pelosi, J., and Dixon, R.T. *How to Monitor Agencies Serving Children.* Durham, N.C.: LINC Press, 1974.

Lindsley, O. From Skinner to precision teaching: The child knows best. In J.B. Jordan and L.S. Robbins (Eds.), *Let's Try Doing Something Else Kind of Thing.* Arlington, Va.: Council for Exceptional Children, 1972.

Patterson, G.R., and Harris, A. Some methodological considerations for observation procedures. Unpublished manuscript. University of Oregon, Eugene.

Pelosi, J., and Johnson, S.L. *Advocacy for Your Child.* Durham, N.C.: LINC Press, 1974.

Perske, R., and Marquiss, J. Learning to live in an apartment: Retarded adults from institutions and dedicated citizens. *Mental Retardation,* 1973, *11(5),* 18.

Reid, J.B. Reliability assessment of observation data: A possible methodological problem. Unpublished manuscript, University of Wisconsin, Madison.

7

Examining Consumers' Assumptions

H. Rutherford Turnbull, III, and Ann P. Turnbull

Ann P. Turnbull and H. Rutherford Turnbull III are the parents of a moderately retarded eleven-year old boy, Jay. Together they have recently edited *Parents Speak Out: Views from The Other Side of the Two-Way Mirror,* a collection of essays by parents of developmentally disabled children—but parents who are professionals in the DD field. They also are former officers and directors of group homes, sheltered workshops, and county associations for retarded citizens, as well as of a state-wide coalition of parents and professionals for handicapped children. Professionally they are the coauthors of a recent book, *Free Appropriate Public Education: Law and Implementation,* about federal right-to-education laws and court decisions.

Ann is a special educator on the faculty of the University of North Carolina and is the author of two recent books about special education, *Developing and Implementing Individualized Educational Programs* and *Mainstreaming Handicapped Students: A Guide for the Classroom Teacher.* Rud is a lawyer on the faculty of the same university and drafted North Carolina's recently enacted limited guardianship law and special education law. He serves on the governmental affairs committee of National Association for Retarded Citizens, is vice-president (Legal Process Subdivision) of the American Association on Mental Deficiency, and has been chairman of that Association's legal and social issues committee for two years.

About three years ago, while writing in *The New York Times* about our retarded son, Jay, we laid down a simple axiom for parents of retarded children: we cannot make the same assumptions about our handicapped children that parents quite freely make about their nonhandicapped children. We have given this axiom considerable thought since then and now venture another axiom: one should always examine one's own assumptions and the assumptions others hold, especially when advocating for handicapped children and adults.

For example, we make different assumptions about our two nonhandicapped daughters than we do about Jay:

1. Our daughters will have a public education, and we expect it will be generally appropriate. Although our son has a right to an appropriate

education, guaranteed by federal and state laws, we cannot simply assume that the legal guarantee will be effectuated;

2. Our daughters will directly benefit from many public recreation programs. Although it is true that Jay can enroll in a limited number of programs as a matter of right, his meaningful participation cannot be taken for granted. We still have to be vigilant in assuring that he is enrolled and integrated into the activities;

3. Our daughters will have socialization opportunities which will be self-initiated and relatively easy to establish, blending into the normal experiencies of their peer groups and social setting. To a large extent, Jay's socialization will have to be contrived, and he will always be a "curiosity object" to many people within the community;

4. Our daughters will be served by public health services and hospitals. Although state and federal laws provide that Jay may not be excluded from such services because he is handicapped, we know that the absence of people in those programs who can accommodate Jay's handicap (as distinguished from being able to treat his disease or broken fingers) is a major barrier to his receiving services there;

5. Our daughters will, in the normal course of events, go to college, find jobs, and establish their own residence and their own families. Although there are adult education programs for retarded people, they are scant and primarily vocationally-related; Jay's prospects to work in noncompetitive settings are hardly cheering; his and our choice of congregate living settings is limited (although increasing); and his chances for nonrelated-family ties are almost utterly serendipitous unless he is admitted into a coeducational group home.

In short, Jay's legal rights to education and nondiscriminatory access to public service and his opportunities for "normalization" as a human being are still such a long way from being fulfilled that we continue to have to make assumptions for Jay that are markedly different than we may make for our daughters.

There are, as well, political complications that make it risky to indulge assumptions about Jay and other handicapped people. Recent national concerns about inflation (and the concommitant reduction in federal funding of human services projects), the omnipresent Proposition 13 mentality, the "conservative" trend of the 1978 Congressional elections, and the no longer covert or polite reaction to federal and state governmental regulation all tend to make the coming years particularly hard ones for advocates for developmentally disabled persons. One cannot assume that new rights or benefits will be created or that existing ones will be fully recognized by federal or state legislatures or executive agencies.

Moreover, victories won by other handicapped citizens do not always benefit developmentally disabled people, although they frequently are popularly seen as advantageous to all "the handicapped." Public opposition and reaction to each victorious handicapped person often becomes opposition to every "handicapped" person. And, sadly, the victories in too many cases are more symbolic than real. For example, mobility-impaired people are the primary beneficiaries of barrier-free buildings and transportation systems. Some developmentally disabled people also are primary beneficiaries; others, however, are only secondary beneficiaries or will reap no benefits at all because of the nature or severity of their handicaps or because they are constrained in their choices of where they may live. The extensive elevator system in the District of Columbia metro system does not benefit institutionalized nonambulatory retarded people, and some observers feel it is too infrequently used by mentally able mobility-impaired people, causing it to become an unwelcome symbol of hollow victories.

Thus, despite newly-won rights, one cannot assume that the future of developmentally disabled persons is brighter now than before. Politically, the trend of the times and the economy undercut such an assumption. Further, any assumption which may have been made that victory for one group of handicapped people is victory for all and always worth the price is evermore indefensible. Similarly, the deaf college students who "wins" his claim that he must be furnished an interpreter in classrooms or the blind person whose employer is required to furnish readers or brailled company memoranda contributes to the welfare of deaf or blind people, simultaneously making it more expensive for colleges and employers to accommodate other handicapped people, especially those who are not deaf or blind. There are, after all, limitations to public funds and boundaries to public goodwill.

Nonetheless, many "consumer advocates" continue to make assumptions about retarded, otherwise developmentally disabled, or other handicapped people. We think it would be useful to set out some of those assumptions made by advocates for the handicapped and the contrary or divergent assumptions that are often made by people outside the "consumer advocacy" movement. Such an exercise is of more than academic value, for it may contribute to sharpening advocacy skills and becoming more thoughtful about even our most fundamental assumptions.

Parent and professional advocates might assume that handicapped people's rights are self-executing. "Society" may know otherwise and sometimes require that advocates make rights meaningful in the political arena (especially on appropriations issues) and courts (as in the case of noncompliance with education rights) to reestablish what the law had already specified.

Advocates might assume that rights won in one arena (such as due process in public education) will beget equally useful rights in other areas (such as due process in the parents' placement of minors in institutions). Due process, however, is a Draconian sword: public educators may use it to take the offensive against handicapped students, and not all aspects of a handicapped person's life are equally suitable to due process being applied—after all, the state's control over a child in a school setting is quite different than its interest in regulating family decisions about placement of minors.

Advocates might assume that handicapped people can always be treated in the same way as nonhandicapped people. While it is perfectly true that there are vast areas of common characteristics of handicapped and nonhandicapped people and that equal treatment is warranted, it is likewise true that there are marked dissimilarities and consequently bona fide reasons for dissimilar treatment. The differences have not escaped society's notice, and many persons outside the "DD field" assume that dissimilarity is the general rule.

In a related vein, advocates perhaps assume that handicapped people can learn, work gainfully, and conform to social mores. In turn, they assume that handicapped people are important teachers to the nonhandicapped (they instruct others how to respect differences) and that handicapped people should, therefore, be integrated with nonhandicapped people. When integrated, it is believed that handicapped people will be better able to learn, have employment opportunities, and begin to adhere to social norms. Yet it is unfortunate but true that some handicapped people are severely limited in their learning, work, and conforming capacities; it may not necessarily follow that they should be fully integrated, either for their own or others' benefit. One may not assume that society, in general, believes in the integration principle. If anything, when people are free to choose with whom they associate, they tend to associate with people like themselves.

The integration assumption may lead advocates to assume that the failure to integrate the handicapped person with nonhandicapped people represents a social failure that government must remedy. This assumption may encourage the belief that "society" is obligated to handicapped people, that society may not properly consider the cost of its obligation, and that society must, in short order, make all of the accommodations that all handicapped people need, whatever the cost and without regard to the competing interests that exist within the full spectrum of handicapped populations and between the handicapped and the nonhandicapped.

"Society," on the other hand, may believe that it is not cost effective for them to pay to accommodate handicapped people; they may even attribute the responsibility for the handicapping condition to the fathers and mothers (and in this they sometimes are correct, particularly with respect to genetically related retardation or fetal alcohol syndrome children, for example); and thus, they may contend that the responsible persons have lifetime obligations to their children and that society has none.

Finally, some advocates may be tempted to assume that single-issue politics is both desirable and profitable: desirable because it is a single-minded (and thus simple or simplistic) approach to complex issues, and profitable because one's "friends" and "enemies" can be easily classified for support or defeat. Nothing is so clear, however, as the enormous complexity of the politics of developmental disabilities; convoluted political considerations do not easily lend themselves to single-issue politics, nor should they. Only absolute rules may be able to luxuriate in pure dichotomies of "friends" and "enemies."

Effective consumer advocates are ones who know and have examined what they and others assume, are prepared to modify their assumptions in light of facts and to adduce facts that make others modify their assumptions, and only very cautiously indulge in any assumptions at all. Developmentally disabled children and adults, their parents, and their advocates already have made too many arguable or doubtful assumptions. Advocacy does not need true believers, people who, in Eric Hoffer's incandescent words, have lost sight of their goals. One way to keep one's goals in sight, we believe, is to deal rigorously with assumptions, both those of the advocates and those of society. As consumer advocates examine assumptions, they should be able to focus their goals more sharply, plan how to achieve them, and move successfully toward their accomplishments. And that is effective consumer advocacy.

8
Legal Advocacy for Developmentally Disabled People

Donald O. Mayer

All persons born or naturalized in the United States, and subject to the
jurisdiction thereof, are citizens of the United States and of the State wherein
they reside. No State shall make or enforce any law which shall abridge the
principles, privileges, or immunities of the citizens of the United States, nor
shall any State deprive any person of life, liberty, or property without *due
process* of law, nor deny to any person within its jurisdiction the *equal
protection* of the laws.
(Constitution of the United States, Amendment XIV, 1868). Emphasis
added.

The Constitution of the United States lays down the most fundamental
principles for the organization and administration of our society. The concepts
of equal protection and due process contained in the Fourteenth Amendment
embody basic moral principles of fundamental fairness. Not only must the
laws be applied equally to diverse groups within the society, but, where
deliberate classifications or exclusions are embodied in legislation, whether
state or federal, a compelling governmental interest must exist to justify such
a classification or exclusion. Both the equal protection and due process
clauses have been cited in numerous cases involving the rights of individuals
civilly committed to public institutions for treatment or habilitation: the right
to have various state standards relating to, for example, fire safety and food
sanitation equally applied to residential institutions; the right to equal educational opportunity; and the right to be free from inappropriate educational
classification, labelling and placement.

Other constitutional provisions such as the Eighth Amendment's prohibi-
tion against cruel and unusual punishment, and the Thirteenth Amendment's
proscription against involuntary servitude have been invoked in lawsuits on
behalf of developmentally disabled people. No attempt is here made to further
explain these constitutional concepts or their development in litigation on

behalf of developmentally disabled people. Several excellent sources which can be used to refresh or extend the reader's familiarity are listed in the Selected Bibliography.

As an introduction and background to discussion of legal advocacy techniques, the writer believes it worthwhile to reflect upon why it has taken a century for these various constitutional principles to be applied to the problems of developmentally disabled people. While granting that money spent for the education of culturally deprived children may be a reasonable investment for the future, many citizens may regard money spent for education of developmentally disabled people a waste of resources. Implicit in such a view is the importance of an investment from an economic standpoint; that is, at a time when this country needs to marshall its resources to maintain its military and economic leadership, we cannot afford to "fritter away" taxpayers' money just to teach the handicapped to go to the toilet. In a society which prizes the most intelligent, attractive, and powerful, there is minimal public concern or sympathy for those without all these natural advantages. As Turnbull (1975) has stated, "We have traditionally resorted to Social Darwinism in law and economics, with the wholly predictable result that the developmentally disabled have been the ultimate and inevitable losers."

By focusing on "survival of the fittest" as a prevailing ethic, the intent is not to explain all important aspects of social organization, but rather to identify a predominant force at work against the developing movement for dignity and equal rights for the disabled. "Rights" are typically conferred by the common consent of the governed, and such consent largely depends upon the prevailing social conscience. The writer believes that in the absence of active and effective legal intervention on behalf of disabled people, the vast majority of citizens will continue to be satisfied with the status quo.

Further, satisfaction is guaranteed when people can point to an institution and somehow believe that the state is taking good care of the disabled, even though this belief is not founded upon observation of actual conditions. Unless families can find some financial and psychological support in the local community, they will continue to be forced to resort to state institutionalization as the means of caring for their disabled members. But institutionalization represents essentially a nonsolution: The parent's role easily becomes one of financial support and infrequent visitation; and, for the disabled citizen, life within the institution brings about a fundamental and permanent change. The analogy between prisons and residential centers for the disabled may seem overplayed, but similarity is clearly evident in the inability of residents to adjust to non-institutional norms after a year or more within the institution. The basic thrust of normalization as a goal in the treatment of developmentally disabled people in institutions is to counteract this process and to provide maximum opportunities for development. Institutions, removed as they are from the mainstream of life, provide inherently limited opportunities for residents. But no listing of institutional shortcomings can be as convincing as one unguided tour of a residential center for severely retarded people.

Advocacy for equality is not strictly a matter of defining the legal rights of developmentally disabled citizens and establishing groups to insure these rights. The growth of "legal rights" for developmentally disabled people is but a part of the continuing movement to bring about fundamental change in public and private attitudes and actions. This movement should result in the restoration of many developmentally disabled people to a useful and dignified place in the community. It is the writer's opinion that the continued existence of large scale state institutions is antithetical to this movement. Paving the way for a gradual transition to communities requires that state Developmental Disabilities Councils both provide leadership in formulating new directions and share their findings with other state Councils. Advocacy that works to achieve governmental consideration of the needs of developmentally disabled citizens at every level and advocacy that promotes their individuality and dignity will also work to insure equality and fairness.

A favorable climate for informed legal advocacy has been created by various Federal judicial decisions, Congressional legislation, and Federal agency regulations. In adition, numerous states have been actively revising outdated codes and providing for better procedures to protect the rights of disabled people. Thus, State agencies and state institutions must now conform not only to Constitutional standards but also to an increasing barrage of laws and regulations directed at insuring better lives for developmentally disabled citizens.

The remainder of this chapter will focus primarily on legal advocacy in three related settings:

1. The institution,
2. the community, and
3. the state.

This does not imply that continuing efforts to secure beneficial legislation or favorable Federal court rulings are now less urgent.

ADVOCACY IN THE INSTITUTION

The level of care at existing residential facilities should be monitored in accordance with applicable accreditation or regulatory standards. In some states, voluntary (consumer) agencies are performing this function with strong community-based advocates aware of significant regulations. For example, HEW regulations require a plan of compliance from a residential facility for mentally retarded citizens prior to commission of significant support funds under

Title XIX (Medicaid), funds which may be crucial to the continued viability of the institution. An advocacy group might elect to assist the facility in anticipating such standards by alerting it to problem areas. Alternately, acceptance and use of funds without substantial compliance could conceivably render the institution liable in damages, either to the individuals as intended beneficiaries or to the federal government on a breach of contract theory.

Holding institutions accountable involves more than the application of national standards to facilities and living conditions. More than anything else, strong support from lay advocates is needed, and several states (Minnesota is a good example) have concerned citizens acting as lay advocates at institutions. Intervention on behalf of disabled clients at this level often results in a new awareness on the part of institutional employees and administrators that the disabled, too, have rights and entitlements. Citizen groups, along with parents, social workers, and other professionals, are the best source of information about what is going on in institutions.

If there is no active citizen organization, the possibility of establishing a legal advocacy program in the institution should be considered. The states of Washington, New Jersey, and North Carolina have pioneered this type of advocacy. The virtues are several: they provide intervention at the basic level; they are working to insure that individual residents receive what is rightfully theirs; and they provide for direct intervention by one person on behalf of another.

Some typical legal issues at the institutional level include: lack of individualized treatment or habilitation programs; the use of questionable therapies, such as seclusion or the use of mild electric shock, guardianship, transfer to other institutions; and issues of normalization such as privacy, mail, visitors, storage space, etc. The American Bar Association report on the Washington State Mental Health-Retardation Legal Services Project also lists social security questions, consumer matters, and criminal matters as principal problems to be dealt with at the institutional level. It should be noted that nonlawyers can be quite effective as advocates, but that some legal support structures are needed to provide up-to-date information on applicable legislation or regulations, as well as to lend occasional assistance in negotiations or potential litigation.

Whether lawyers or non-lawyers are used as institutional advocates, one frequent problem will be the difficulty of establishing a bond of trust between the advocate and the residential client who, quite understandably, may be unwilling to confide in one who appears to be another administrator. In addition, professionals will inevitably come into conflict with an advocate over issues such as experimentation, use of aversive stimuli or seclusion to effect behavioral change, or the lack of individual treatment plans. While such conflicts are not to be avoided, advocates must have some assurance of institutional support to have any leverage on these issues. Here again, the existence of legal support structures is enormously helpful: not only will professionals tend to give more respect to the opinions and recommendations of another professional, but the possibility of a potential lawsuit on more serious issues injects a powerful antidote to resistance to change. Finally, advocates embroiled in day-to-day conditions of institutional life may find it difficult to keep up with the wealth of legal materials now being generated in the field of "mental health law." A state-wide legal group could alert advocates to the more significant legal developments.

Clearly, such state-sponsored programs have potential problems, but where state-wide citizen groups have not actively intervened, state DD Councils should determine if they can provide any support or encouragement to such groups. In addition, Councils may recommend to county civil groups to set as their goal the sponsorship of the legal rights of disabled citizens at a nearby institution. Individuals assigned to particular residents can assess their needs and rights and intervene where needs are unmet or rights violated.

ADVOCACY IN THE COMMUNITY

None of the foregoing is intended to suggest that legal advocacy should primarily take place at institutions. In fact, many lawyers working in the field of mental health law believe that institutional advocacy can effect only marginal improvements in a basically restricted environment. Community advocates are needed to pave the way for a gradual transition from the dominance of custodial care to the prevalence of more comprehensive community support services for disabled citizens and their families. In many instances, the lack of such services necessitates commitment to an institution. Thus community advocacy would include not only the establishment of local supports for disabled citizens and their families, but also legal confrontation with local authorities wrongfully withholding benefits from disabled citizens or excluding them from community life.

Legal confrontation can come on a variety of issues: for example, securing educational rights from local public school systems; securing all entitlements from local offices of state and federal agencies; providing rehabilitation rather than criminal penalties or incarceration for mentally retarded juvenile offenders; assuring equal access to public buildings and transportation systems, and confronting municipal officials on restrictive zoning ordinances designed to keep out group home or halfway houses. Just as community law advocates have worked both within the community and at institutions, institutional advocates, or a statewide support structure, could assist community groups with legal confrontation. This may be especially desirable where community politics makes it difficult for neighbors to bring legal actions against neighbors. Community and institutional advocates must work together where possible, to insure that the needs of all developmentally disabled citizens are met in the least restrictive way possible.

Community advocates can lead the way in suggesting the establishment of group homes and the formulation of appropriate programs eligible for federal aid under Title 20 of the Social Security Act or other funding sources. Recent amendments to that Act, specifically Section 2001, authorize annual appropriations to encourage each state to furnish services directed at the goal of preventing or reducing inappropriate institutional care by providing for community based care, home based care, or other forms of less "intensive" care. Perhaps the DD Council could disseminate information to various key audiences describing the successes or failures of some of the more unique or promising programs.

For the use of in-state advocates, a referral and information program on community services throughout the state should be established. Pilot projects that have proven unusually successful should be expanded to other counties in order to provide more comprehensive coverage. At the community level, the lack of comprehensive support services is ultimately the major barrier against deinstitutionalization of significant numbers of developmentally disabled residents. A continuing and important advocacy function of the state DD Council could thus be to establish and monitor community programs which meet these needs.

Vital work is presently being done by community advocates in referral and information areas, as well as in running interference for clients facing the system at a crucial time. For example, in presenting a child for admittance to public educational programs, the advocate can assist parents by familiarizing them with procedures necessary to "protect the case for subsequent appeal": if a negative reply is given to a request, find out why, demand an explanation in writing; record names, dates, times, and places. Several advocates report that such stratagems are necessary in that many bureaucrats will tend to give the answer that provides the least effort on their own part. Even where they appear most certain they may be actually mistaken about the content of their own regulations or directives. Moreover, the system is more responsive to those who are prepared to wrestle with it.

ADVOCACY AT THE STATE LEVEL

Confronting the system is most effective when the system as a whole is understood. The various laws and regulations responding to the needs of developmentally disabled people are often complex and detailed. Specialists at the state level are needed to constantly sift through written material and to provide the relevant considerations for local advocates. Additionally, a specialist could suggest possible resolutions and strategies related to legal problems in accordance with their understanding of "the system" as a whole. Such understanding would comprehend the structure of the bureaucracy, and such a system could not, of course, be constructed on a three-year grant. Ideally, those interested in legal advocacy for the disabled will attempt to find some means of establishing a structure independent of government grants.

Legal aid clinics, Bar association committees, and public interest action groups can assist local advocacy, but for a variety of reasons cannot provide any ongoing leadership for local advocacy. Primarily, this lack of leadership capacity stems from (1) the fact that "mental health law" has become a specialized and rapidly developing field of legal interest, so that nearly full-time interest must be devoted to keeping up with it, and (2) the fact that understanding "the system" in any particular state also requires inside information that only becomes accessible to a specialist after a certain number of years. Local legal aid clinics still supported by Federal funds to some degree, have various requirements as to client population and types of cases which generally inhibit the development of a complete specialist at the local level. Still, many legal aid attorneys may have an interest in the rights of developmentally disabled citizens, and this interest may be nurtured by the existence of a state-wide legal advocacy group which could conduct seminars and workshops on the latest legal developments. More significantly local advocates could be referred to interested legal aid attorneys for the purpose of bringing administrative appeals or filing a lawsuit.

The capability to bring a lawsuit is an essential safeguard of anyone's rights and in view of the present condition of legal rights for developmentally disabled people, such capability is necessary to balance the "take it or leave it" tendencies of many state and federal agencies. For an excellent discussion of litigation as an agent for legal change, consult the booklet *Legal Change for the Handicapped Through Litigation* published by the State Federal Information Clearing House for Exceptional Children, and edited by Alan Abeson. In brief, it should be noted that the potential to bring a lawsuit is a vital element in any negotiating process and that constructive change can often be achieve through confrontation with agencies which would greatly prefer not to be involved in or on the losing side of a public lawsuit.

In some cases, national organizations such as the Mental Health Law Project, in Washington, D.C., may be willing to handle cases that promise to provide valuable precedent for future actions. Also, the National Center for Law and the Handicapped in South Bend, Indiana, is a potentially valuable resource with extensive case files on many significant legal actions on behalf of the developmentally disabled.

However, the lack of in-state attorneys active in law for the handicapped is a serious disadvantage, as state agencies may respond only when commanded by a "higher" authority such as the legislature, or a federal or state appellate level court, and may feel no urgency whatever to respond where advocates are too disorganized to bring a clearly justified lawsuit. State DD Councils are for various reasons not ideally positioned to bring lawsuits, for their function is planning and advising, not litigating. But the existence of some effective legal advocacy group with that capability is essential to a comprehensive plan to insure the legal rights of developmentally disabled people.

Several states have initiated such groups. In New Jersey a Department of Public Advocacy was created in essense to sue the State when necessary. In New York the Developmental Disabilities Council has begun a legal advocacy program funded partly with DD funds and partly with funds from the New York State Association for Retarded Children. The New York program has the two vital elements: capability for class action litigation and training for community organizing. In Minnesota, the state ARC has created an entirely independent legal advocacy group with litigation capability, as well as a strong emphasis on the training of lay advocates. Their training manual is available at a nominal cost. In Colorado as well, successful legal advocacy reportedly rests upon vigorous and informed advocacy at the community level by citizen groups. Finally, the Iowa DD Council has established a standing committee whose focus is legal advocacy.

More recently as a result of the 1975 and 1978 Developmental Disability Acts state level legal advocacy groups with litigation and training potential have been developed in every state. These systems have varied functions which include:

1. providing legal aid attorneys with specialized knowledge in the areas of law for the handicapped;
2. working with state consumer groups to help formulate training programs for lay advocates;
3. maintaining close liaison with legislators, many of whom are also attorneys;
4. providing continuity in relations with state agencies and bar organizations; and
5. helping evaluate legislative and administrative proposals.

CONCLUSION

It is understood that few state DD Councils will be able to implement quickly a complete advocacy program where one is not already in existence. The elements of such a program include both informed local advocates in the communities and in residential institutions and a state wide legal advocacy resource. Local and institution based advocates can monitor institutional standards, intervene on issues of improper treatment, propose and maintain effective support structures in the community which take care of the needs of developmentally disabled people and their families without resort to institutions, and help insure that local arms of state agencies, including the public school system, are giving the disabled citizens their full legal entitlement. Ultimately a well designed state-wide legal advocacy program can serve as a resource to assist local advocates on legal issues and can provide a capability for bringing lawsuits and administrative appeals where necessary.

REFERENCES

Legal Change for the Handicapped Through Litigation, Alan Abeson, ed., State-Federal Information Clearinghouse for Exceptional Children, Reston, VA.

"Through and Beyond the History of the Mentally Retarded," Rutherford Turnbull in *Advocacy: A Role for DD Councils,* James L. Paul, Ron Wiegerink, G. Ronald Neufeld, eds. Published in 1975 by DD/TAS, Room 300, NCNB Plaza, Chapel Hill, NC 27514.

Developmentally Disabled Assistance and Bill of Rights Act (PL 94-103).

Developmental Disability Act (PL 95-602).

9

Self-Advocacy
and Changing Attitudes

Rita A. Varela

What are society's attitudes toward the disabled person? How can those of us who are concerned with public awareness change them? Are they changing already, without our help or control, as a result of the disabled self-advocacy movement? We cannot even begin to tackle these questions until we examine the relationship between people and the rehabilitation service delivery system.

SPECIAL PROCESSING

Disabled citizens are probably the most counseled people in America. They are, indeed, a managed community. Although our society prides itself on its willingness to help the handicapped, the mechanisms it has created to dispense its benevolence have—at times subtlely and at times, as in the case of certain custodial care institutions, brutally (Wolfensberger, 1974)—worked to suppress assertiveness and self-determination. Some disabled citizens do slip into the mainstream without help. Most, however, find that in order to get into the educational system, the health care system, and the income systems (jobs or government income maintenance) they must submit to special processing. From the time their difference is first diagnosed and noted they become legitimate targets for counseling and advice. They are constantly exposed to the same, negative message: "You've got to be fixed up." In the course of the processing they become exiled, sometimes permanently, into a world of special doctors, special teachers, and special counselors who have been assigned to do the fixing. This processing has a profound impact both on the self-concept of disabled people and on society's view of them.

For the disabled person, processing means being set apart: bouncing in, out, and through countless programs, evaluations, agencies, and clinics, only to return, each time, to a sundered path, adjacent to society yet never with it, forever gazing toward the city from the woods, and confined, condemned like Sisyphus, to a road that veers from life. What gives this a political dimension is that it is not on a road at all but on a bureaucratic conveyor belt. The route is predestined by bias and by a network of laws and agencies, which rule that if you are born or become disabled you automatically fall under an alternative set of procedures. The network is man-made and alterable. Disabled children have not been put in special classes to satisfy the laws of physics but, rather, the laws of the state. Parents, furthermore, can have a lot of influence on the legislature when they get fed up and start organizing.

Still, the very magnitude of the processing system is oppressive. Without realizing it, disabled persons do, at least in part, begin to accept the assumption that there is something wrong with them and that human service personnel have a right to intervene. Yet chances are that the consumer has gone to a great many fixers through the years and still has big problems: no job, no transportation, no accessible housing. Some of the counselors may have even proposed conflicting remedies. What we have, then, is a client who has received too much negative feedback to trust himself and not enough positive rewards to trust the specialists.

THE SELLING OF THE DISABLED

For society, the special processing means that somebody—somebody *else*—is handling disabled people and that there is no need for the average, nondisabled citizen to deal with them or be concerned about what is going on. Many people hear about disability issues primarily through telethons and public service announcements, and consumers have not always been pleased at the way these vehicles portray them. Too often, telethons have sought to merchandize the disabled child, who is generally depicted as cute, helpless, and somewhat pathetic. Sometimes telethons have also tried to sell the horror of disability, and the audience has had to watch as the celebrity host wipes a tear from his eye and tells them that if their children are normal they should thank God everyday (CYCP, 1976).

Public service announcements are far less maudlin, and do, undoubtedly, convey important information. Disabled persons and their families should know about community referral services and rehabilitation centers. Yet the PSAs also tend to reinforce the traditional perspective by telling the public that: a) there is something special out there that has been set aside to handle those people and b) if you support such ventures—either by giving money to a charity or by giving passive approval to a government-sponsored program—you are off the hook. The pity, the helplessness, and the horror of disability, when presented in conjunction with scenes of bright, shiny, photogenic offices filled with up-to-date equipment to deliver topnotch services, work to justify the special processing and exile. It is neither the telethons nor the PSAs themselves that are deplorable, but rather the absence of a second and more objective correlative between the lives of disabled people and what we are told about this population. Where is Judy Heumann, who started Disabled in Action, who led civil rights demonstrations, and who was carried off an airplane and arrested simply because she uses a wheelchair? Where is Frank Bowe, director of the American Coalition of Citizens with Disabilities, who works 60 and 70 hours a week to ensure that the voices of disabled Americans are heard in Washington, D. C.? Where are the millions of others, who remain unknown but who work and pay taxes, who struggle and dream, who have babies, who get divorced, who die without finishing their novel? No, we are not told about them. Telethons and PSAs are carefully designed to perform very specific functions, which, ultimately, are supposed to make it easier for disabled individuals to get along in society. Unfortunately, the picture they draw is rather alien and sterile, and often confirms the suspicion that people like that are not kin to a world like this.

SELF-ADVOCACY AND CHANGING ATTITUDES

The disabled self-advocacy movement represents a growing challenge to these bleak and sterile portraits. True, the movement does not speak with a single voice. It is a large, loud proliferation of leaders from different size groups, some cohesive and some not, that, at first glance, seem to share only their commitment to those whom society has left behind. On closer examination, however, one finds three major themes of consensus.

The first theme is that the fixers are not fixing much and there is a need for new strategies. The human service system, generally, has viewed the problems of education, housing, jobs, and transportation as stemming from the deficits of the client. The client, therefore, had to be altered, made adaptable to the environment. The movement, however, has seen them as problems of access, of a system that is not distributing benefits equitably, and has often sought redress through legislation and the court.

A second theme concerns the attitudes of human service personnel toward disabled persons. Consumers charge that counselors see only the client's disability, not the potential, and that counselors always show a livelier interest in behavior modification than in affirmative action. There is a disturbing amount of evidence indicating that these charges may have some merit. Harold E. Yuker and the staff of the Human Resources Center, in their historic and comprehensive study, found that the attitudes of a rehabilitation worker toward clients tend to become increasingly negative as the years pass (Yuker, Block, and Young, 1970). The study also found that the attitudes of rehabilitation professionals toward the disabled tend to be more negative than do the attitudes of employers, nondisabled co-workers, and nondisabled school peers.

Do these attitudes affect the quality of rehabilitative planning? Some innovators within the profession feel the answer is "yes":

> The vocational rehabilitation of persons with severe disabilities has a long history, a history dominated by an expectancy cycle that perpetuates low levels of success and low employment capabilities.
>
> Virtually all that has been attempted has taken place in the context of simple, menial tasks that require little training, skill or attention. In fact, most program descriptions that are available focus on tasks that are labor intensive rather than machine intensive, thereby accentuating the disabilities rather than the capabilities (United Cerebral Palsy Governmental Activities Office, 1977).

A third and closely related theme concerns self-help. The programs sponsored by Berkeley's Center for Independent Living and Minnesota's United Handicapped Federation are logical extensions of the movement's emphasis on dignity and self-determination. These organizations, and similar ones emerging throughout the country, offer such services as peer counseling, assertiveness training, hot lines, and information and referral. Their members also tend to take an active interest in civic and legislative matters. These, then, are the self-advocates, bringing their case directly to politicians and the press, and refusing to rely exclusively on those specialists and providers who traditionally have served as surrogate spokesmen.

Thus, what we are seeing is a shift in relationships within the human service constituency. The constituency consists of people who have a stake in the status of disabled citizens that encompasses more than one issue and that has lasted or can be expected to last several years. It includes disabled persons, their families, volunteers who have shown a long-term interest in disability issues, and people whose careers are tied to the rehabilitation field. Traditionally, the advocates for disabled Americans have been professionals who, in turn, received moral and financial support from parent activists. Often it was the parents who initiated partnerships with the professional community. Regardless how they were recruited, it has been the professionals who have drawn the plans and priorities; and although parent and consumer power has often been responsible for getting appropriations through Congress, it has been the service providers who have sat down with federal bureaucrats to decide how best to allocate the funds.

As the pressure from the self-advocacy movement has increased, however, some attitudes have changed and so have some rules. We can see the advocate's impact on the Federal-State Vocational Rehabilitation program, for example. For years, consumers have told Congress that VR agencies should be more responsive to consumer views. The success of Berkeley's

Center for Independent Living and similar projects helped buttress arguments for expanding the decision-making process. As a result, state VR agencies must now design and implement plans for consumer involvement (Rehabilitation Services Manual). The developmental disabilities concept is based on similar consumer involvements.

This mandate is yielding mixed results. In some states, the relationship between consumers and state agencies has not been at all cordial. Thus, the partnership envisioned by this mandate has had a slow start. In other states, however, we find agencies funding self-help centers and peer counseling, and find consumer advisory groups working with professionals to design pilot projects, rewrite client complaint procedures, and present budget requests to the legislature.

NEW PERSPECTIVES

Richman and Trohanis' (1977) *Perspectives on Public Awareness* attempts to examine the relation between perspectives toward disabled persons and the mission of rehabilitative planning in order to offer guidance to those involved in awareness campaigns. With self-advocates gaining the attention of politicians, the courts, and the press, the task of influencing public attitudes becomes rather complex, simply because the traditionalists and the new activists are presenting different views of reality. We do not have sufficient evidence to gauge the impact that these conflicting messages have on the public. Within the human service constituency, however, we see that as the power centers shift, expand, and contract, people are getting on each others' nerves.

This tension will affect not only those responsible for public information, but everyone in disability-related work. What can public relations specialists and awareness advocates do? First, we must realize that guidelines, although important, have limits. Responding to issues, which can be done by circulating "thou shall not" lists, is not enough. We must address the mission, which is both constant and ever growing. The process, the expanding constituency itself, is the problem, and unless individuals respond to that change they are not responding at all. Just as disabled people must be allowed to participate in policy making and service delivery, they must also become partners in public advocacy. The point is not that you can buy off militants by putting one of them on a campaign committee. The point is that unless we can treat each other as equals we don't know what we're talking about.

Today's consumers tend to have a small voice within the human service field. Planning is still done for disabled citizens, not with them. Yet things are changing. If the number of assertive consumers within the constituency continues to expand, if consumers continue improving their media and organizing skills, if self-help projects continue to multiply, and if disabled individuals become more visible members of society, there will be a wearing away of traditional resistance, and professionals will sense increasingly that it is time to consider new perspectives.

REFERENCES

American Coalition of Citizens with Disabilities. *The Coalition*. Washington, D.C., 1977.

Concerned Youth for Cerebral Palsy. CYCP position paper on telethons. New York: United Cerebral Palsy Association, Inc., September, 1976.

Key, V.O., Jr. *Politics, Parties, and Pressure Groups*. 5th Ed. New York: Thomas Y. Crowell Co., 1964.

Rehabilitation Services Manual. Policy development consultation, Chapter 25. Washington, D.C.: DHEW Rehabilitation Services Administration.

Richman, G., and Trohanis, P. *Perspectives on Public Awareness*. Chapel Hill, N.C.: Frank Porter Graham Child Development Center, 1977.

United Cerebral Palsy Governmental Activities Office. Statement on the need for increased federal efforts related to early education of disabled young children, and for applied technology to meet individual needs of severely disabled adults. Testimony submitted to the Subcommittee on the Handicapped, U.S. Senate Committee on Labor and Public Welfare, Ross E. Clarke, Ronald S. Torner, and G. Gordon Williamson. Washington, D.C., February 25, 1977.

Wolfensberger, S. *The Origin and Nature of Our Institutional Models*. Syracuse: Human Policy Press, 1974.

Yuker, H.E., Block, J.R., and Young, J.H. *The Measurement of Attitudes Toward Disabled Persons*, Chapter 7. Albertson, N.Y.: Human Resources Center, 1970.

Part III
PUBLIC AWARENESS

Part III includes three chapters that discuss how public awareness techniques can be used to confront attitude and information barriers that impede services for persons with developmental disabilities.

In "Public Awareness as a Developmentally Disability," Gary Richman and Pascal Trohanis cite lack of public awareness as a substantial barrier to effective provision of services for the developmentally disabled and as such a barrier to Council effectiveness. Although increased other-advocacy public awareness is a major goal for many DD Councils and groups, the authors identify and elaborate on three problem areas, or stumbling blocks, related to public awareness activities. They then describe a number of characteristics that seem to be common to the more successful public awareness efforts.

"Beyond the Sixty-Second Solution," by Laurence Wiseman, provides an examination of two key questions related to public awareness activities: "How can we make what we are doing to change attitudes work better?" and "How will we know when we have done it?" Wiseman discusses each of these questions by raising several key issues and describes the experience of others in terms of what has worked and what has not worked. He concludes by stressing the importance of evaluating public awareness activities.

The final chapter in this part, "Vermont 'Project Awareness'," by Toby Knox, describes the experience of one Council that worked effectively in the area of public awareness. The chapter provides many helpful ideas to be considered in developing and carrying out a program of public awareness.

10

Public Awareness as a Developmental Disability

Gary Richman and Pascal Trohanis

A NEW DEFINITION FOR AN OLD PROBLEM

Developmental Disabilities Councils have a series of complex and challenging tasks. Federal legislation (PL 95-602) mandates them to plan the comprehensive network of the services needed by persons with developmental disabilities, coordinate and integrate an existing fragmented service system, monitor and evaluate the delivery of services, and serve as advocates on behalf of these citizens. Over the past 8 years, as DD Councils have organized to implement these mandates, they have consistently identified one barrier to services for the developmentally disabled. This barrier has become a recurrent theme regardless of what "role" the Council pursues or what goal the Council wishes to accomplish. This barrier existed when Councils first organized in 1971 and persists today, and, to paraphrase the legislative definition of a developmental disability, this condition can be expected to continue throughout our lifetime and is a substantial handicap to the development of a humane system of services for persons with special needs caused by epilepsy, mental retardation, autism, and cerebral palsy. The barrier is the lack of public awareness, knowledge, and sensitivity to the rights and needs of persons with a developmental disability. Regardless of the issue one looks at—medical care, housing, information and referral, education, or transportation—there are invariably people whose attitudes DD Councils would like to change or whose knowledge or information they would like to increase or correct.

DD Councils have consistently identified negative or ambivalent attitudes and lack of or incorrect information as major barriers. As a result they have identified public awareness as a priority goal, attempted to design appropriate strategies and materials, and allocated resources to public awareness activities. Our experiences during the past 6 years providing technical assistance to DD Councils to meet their broad, general mandates and in their specific public awareness activities provide a vantage point from which to share some observations about Councils and public awareness efforts. These observations are of two types. First, there are three interrelated problem areas that seem to be chronic stumbling blocks confronted by most DD Councils. Second, there are a number of characteristics that are common to most of the more successful and rewarding Council public awareness efforts.

Before going further, it is probably worth issuing a caveat: These observations on basic problem areas and characteristics of effectiveness of Councils' public awareness efforts are just observations. They are not based on any particular survey or any formal research on DD Council behavior. Rather, this is the product of several years of observation and work with at least 40 state DD Councils.

SOME STUMBLING BLOCKS

Where do DD Councils stumble? Frequently on the very first step: defining public awareness. This is not to suggest that a formal, academic definition of public awareness is needed, nor is one being offered. Much of the attraction of the term *public awareness* is its generalness and flexibility; it covers a vast array of situations and strategies involved in changing attitudes or information levels. The problem is that *public awareness* conjures up some type of definition, function, or activity in nearly everyone's mind, and almost as often these notions about public awareness tend to restrict the concept to some definite set of functions or activities. While one person sees "public awareness" as the promotion of the DD Council in order to increase its visibility, someone else envisions a statewide mass media campaign, a third person thinks of some type of information and referral hotline or directory of services, and yet another has in mind some type of outreach.

It may seem like a case of "stating the obvious with a profound sense of discovery" to suggest that Council members must agree on a mutually understood definition of public awareness before they can communicate even with each other. Yet a Council may spend considerable time working on just such a definition of deinstitutionalization, respite care, or advocacy, but everyone, it is assumed, knows what public awareness is. That is precisely the problem: everyone does!

The second stumbling block is often a consequence of the plethora of individual notions about what public awareness is. It could be called the "public awareness strategy knee-jerk reflex." It operates like this. Say "public awareness" to anyone and the odds-on response is one of the following: brochure, press release, TV spot, newsletter, or film. These are strategies or techniques to be used in public awareness efforts. Too frequently they become synonymous with public awareness, making the concept of planning public awareness activities meaningless. A Council can easily fulfill a "goal" of having designed and distributed 5,000 brochures by July 1, but that gives no hint of the significance or impact of that action.

It cannot be stressed often enough that public awareness efforts must be planned. The process of planning may be simple or complex, but the Council should be able to answer these five questions:

Who is the target population?

Why do you want to affect them? (If the Council can answer this question by saying they want them to do something, as opposed to know or think something, then they are on the right track.)

What message do they need to receive in order to motivate/enable them to *do* (know/think) it? (The answers to these first three questions comprise a goal statement.)

How are you going to deliver the message? (It is only this fourth question that requires the selection of public awareness techniques to answer.)

How will you know if the target population does/knows/thinks it? (Evaluation! It is also essential that you be able to answer this question as well. Certainly evaluation is essential to account for time and money spent, but there is a more fundamental reason. Public awareness must be more than blindly throwing darts at a wall; there must be a mechanism for seeing if you have hit the target, and preferably the bull's-eye, and then correcting your aim.)

A third stumbling block is a logical consequence of failing to plan public awareness activities appropriately. One of the keys of the developmental disabilities concept is coordination and integration. It is essential that this concept apply to public awareness as well. There is a strong and counter-productive tendency to see public awareness as a separate, discrete endeavor, handled by a specialist, with special techniques. There are two faces to this problem which, when stated, seem painfully obvious; yet, like the first two issues, their existence is found far too frequently. The following scenario illustrates the problem.

A DD Council identifies community resistance as a major barrier to the development of community residences. They develop and fund a general public awareness campaign to change public attitudes concerning persons with developmental disabilities living in the community. At the same time, a state agency or a private service provider is attempting to develop group homes and is meeting substantial opposition in local communities and neighborhoods; they have done no public awareness planning, have no strategy, and are coping with the opposition on a "crisis" basis. It seems obvious that the group home planners need some public awareness effort as part of their strategy if their goal of establishing community residences is to be reached. It should be equally clear that the DD Council has established a strategy but has no real goal. That is, they have failed to adequately address the second question in the planning process, "Why?" Public awareness alone can never lead to the development of group homes. In one form or another these two activities, citing group homes and public awareness relating to community acceptance of the developmentally disabled, are frequently going on independently of each other in one state.

The lesson that must be learned is that public awareness efforts should facilitate program goals. DD Councils consistently identify the public awareness dimensions of problems relating to advocacy, SSI, civil rights, the Education for All Handicapped Children Act (PL 94-142), medical and dental care, community residences, and so on. These are complex problems requiring planned, integrated, and coordinated action on several fronts. Public awareness cannot be the solution, but neither can it be omitted from the solution.

These three stumbling blocks represent the major barriers that Councils must be aware of and overcome. Careful, thoughtful planning and appropriate action should go a long way in helping cope with these potential problems.

CHARACTERISTICS OF SUCCESS

If there are chronic stumbling blocks, there have also been successful and effective public awareness activities. There seem to be a number of characteristics or indicators common to these activities. Certainly they do not constitute a formula for success or effectiveness; there is no "magic bullet" in public awareness. Conversely, these characteristics of success are not a list of minimum prerequisites; some Councils have failed to follow the pattern discussed below or have even done the opposite and still had a significant impact on the public. Nonetheless, the basic characteristics for successful public awareness efforts include surmounting the stumbling blocks and organizing resources in a manner that promotes the integration of public awareness with other program activities.

First, the Council must be able to get beyond the members' individual conceptions of public awareness and reach a mutually understandable definition in order to develop a clear, concise statement of goals and objectives. In practice that has usually meant one, well thought out goal or perhaps two closely related goals. Moreover, this one goal might be characterized as "modest." That is, it has one or more of the following: a limited target audience, limited behavioral objectives, limited message, and can be accomplished within a 1-year plan. This "modest" goal provides a solid foundation of experience, credibility, and self-confidence for the next, more ambitious goal.

The most important indicator of effectiveness concerns the degree to which the public awareness activity is integrated into other program goals. It is possible to identify three general types of DD Council public awareness efforts. In the first type, the Council's goal is self-promotion or self-description. This is typical of new Councils just beginning to think about public awareness and is usually a reaction to their newness and lack of security in the state government landscape. It is generally a sign of Council maturity when the focus of public awareness shifts to the rights and needs of the developmentally disabled.

The second type has as its central theme these rights and needs, but public awareness activities are still largely an isolated, discrete function. In the third type, public·awareness concerning rights and needs is well integrated with other activities that are seeking to assure rights and meet needs. The third type is the strongest indicator of effectiveness.

Do Councils evolve from type two to type three as a maturing or developmental process? Probably not. It is more likely that having progressed beyond type one, a Council employs a public awareness style that is indicative of its general operational style within the state. Councils that are functioning as integrators and coordinators of the service system within the state shape their public awareness efforts similarly. Councils that are isolated and insulated from other organs of state government are probably unable to develop a public awareness or any other kind of activity that is not separate and isolated. The more fundamental problem is nurturing a Council that serves as a coordinator and integrator in all its activities, not just public awareness.

The allocation and organization of resources for public awareness is another characteristic that may serve as an indicator of two things: the level of commitment and, again, the amount of integration. The budget is one crude but simple indicator of commitment.

If there is no budget for public awareness or if the functions are delegated to already overworked staff members, the potential for effectiveness is small. Perhaps the best way to measure the budget is in relative terms, since many of the minimum-allotment states have made a little bit of money go a very long way. However, the little bit of money allocated for public awareness is, for them, a substantial financial commitment.

DD Councils have organized their resources for public awareness in a variety of ways: hiring a full-time person, making grants to private nonprofit organizations, or contracting with professional public relations or advertising firms. Each of these configurations has met with some success. The most effective, or more accurately, least consistently troublesome arrangement has been a staff person supplemented with sufficient budget to "purchase" needed additional expertise. One reason for this is again the notion of integration. The staff person is more directly in touch with the Council, other staff, and other elements of state government and is more able to facilitate a coordinated approach. Similarly, there has been some limited experience but positive results with "grants" to state agencies to add or improve public awareness in ongoing programs.

A final characteristic that indicates both integration and commitment is the involvement of Council members. The potential effectiveness of a Council public awareness staff person is greatly enhanced by an active committee or task force on public awareness. Some Councils who have had effective public awareness programs have used a task group that included resource people with abilities and interests in DD and public awareness who were not necessarily Council members. It is a mutually enhancing cycle when a public awareness effort is interesting and rewarding enough to attract people with the energy and ability to contribute and who are not there due to any commitments implied by membership on the DD Council.

SOME CONCLUDING REMARKS

Public awareness represents a conscious attempt to bring about changes in an audience's knowledge, attitudes, or actions. The awareness effort must be clear, sensitive, and action oriented in its design and approach. Furthermore, the Council must realize that audience changes do not occur overnight. It takes time to overcome ignorance, misinformation, prejudice, and discrimination toward citizens with developmental disabilities. Ultimately, DD Councils must direct their efforts toward the various publics who can and will make a significant difference in the lives of handicapped people.

11

Beyond the Sixty-Second Solution

Laurence Wiseman

> The most important thing to remember is that children and adults who have a degree of mental retardation experience the same feelings, hopes, joys, loves and sorrows that you and I experience. These are qualities that transcend mental and physical handicaps . . . these are the things that make us people.
>
> Vermont Developmental Disabilities
> Planning and Advisory Council

What you have just read is part of a communications campaign undertaken by the Vermont Developmental Disabilities Council. Their goal? To begin to change people's attitudes toward developmentally disabled people. The reason? Negative attitudes toward developmentally disabled people are the props that hold up the barriers between them and the rest of society. All the things that are crucial to a better and more dignified life for people with developmental disabilities—more jobs, more housing, better independent living arrangements—depend, in the end, on how people feel about the developmentally disabled.

Today, according to Frank Bowe, director of the American Coalition of Citizens with Disabilities (ACCD), ''The problem is not so much with us, but with the people who are not disabled. We are always defined in terms of what we cannot do. We are determined to change those attitudes. I want to help others to see us as people, not as crutches and wheelchairs and canes'' (personal communication).

Changing public attitudes toward developmentally disabled people is a vital component of all programs undertaken by DD Councils, so there is little need to justify or rationalize why DD Councils should try to do it. There are two more important questions that need examination. How can we make what we are doing to change attitudes work better? How will we know when we have done it?

DOES IT WORK?

What's good for General Motors is good for the U.S.A.

Charles Wilson

Mr. Wilson was being overly optimistic. While there are points at which the interests of GM and the interests of everybody else clearly intersect, there is at least one area where Mr. Wilson's formula is far off the mark: persuasive communications. What works for General Motors will not work for a human service agency trying to mount successful community education programs. One cannot "sell" developmental disabilities, or prevent drug abuse, or change people's attitudes toward handicapped people the same way GM sells station wagons.

Still, people try to emulate traditional product advertising, and with astonishing results. Many drug prevention programs, for example, were fashioned in the traditional Madison Avenue mold: they relied heavily on television spots, posters, and print. These campaigns not only failed to prevent drug abuse among potential abusers, but a National Institute on Drug Abuse study actually discovered that almost half of those that relied on communicating information had negative impacts. Evidently, learning about drugs—replacing fears and apprehensions with hard facts—did as much to stimulate drug use as it did to inhibit it (Olsen, 1976). The track record of media campaigns to change public attitudes toward developmentally disabled people has been equally disheartening. John Gliedman and William Roth (in press) in "The Grand Illusion: Stigma, Role Expectation and Handicap," go a long way toward explaining why. They examine the sociological underpinnings of attitudes that able-bodied people hold toward people with disabilities. The way able-bodied people relate to disabled people seems to depend on at least three separate factors: inexperience and ignorance; the symbolic overtones of role expectations and/or the handicapped person's inability or unwillingness to fit those stereotypes; and the asymmetry of power relations.

Efforts to change attitudes, therefore, have to be aimed at these three different factors. However, careful aim does not guarantee success. Mass media information campaigns working independently, for example, are generally unable to change attitudes. Richard Ashmore (1975) suggests that their utility is much more limited. They can, he claims, reinforce the feelings of people whose attitudes are already positive, or they can help "justify" attitude and behavior changes in someone whose negative intergroup attitude has been challenged *in some other way*.

Drawing, as Gliedman and Roth do, on an examination of attitudes and behavior toward Blacks, Ashmore suggests that carefully planned, carefully structured direct contact between minority and majority groups is perhaps the most effective mechanism for attitude change. Gliedman and Roth make no such predictions, but they do agree that, to effectively modify public attitudes, we will not only have to modify the tools we are presently using, but we will have to find new tools that will let us chip away at the sociological foundations of prejudice.

Frank Bowe says, "The public image of the handicapped is very heavily weighted toward the telethon/poster child image. We depended on others to do our talking for us. Most often we got just what they were asking for. Charity" (personal communication). Frank Bowe was one of 300 demonstrators who occupied the office of HEW Secretary Joseph A. Califano, Jr., in the spring of 1977. They wanted the Secretary to sign immediately regulations implementing Section 504 of the Rehabilitation Act of 1973. These regulations had come to be known as the "civil rights bill" for handicapped individuals.

The militancy of individuals like Bowe shocked many people. It also forced them to confront their prejudices. While they were used to seeing Blacks or Chicanos or women on the picket lines, wheelchairs and white canes were a novelty. Here were disabled people speaking out on behalf of their own interests. Walter Cronkite called it the beginning of a new civil rights movement. Frank Bowe thinks that it might also be called the beginning of an attitude change campaign that might actually change attitudes about disabled people. William Roth agrees: "Seeing black people in power, in control, did change the way many people perceived blacks. Seeing women in power, in control, did change the way many people perceived women. Perhaps DD Councils should think of what they can do to shape this tool to serve their own attitude change and program goals. Admittedly, there are problems in translating this kind of militancy directly to the DD environment. People who are mentally retarded may still need to depend on advocates who can speak for them. Traditional 'helping' organizations may be initially uncomfortable with clients who do not behave in traditional ways" (Gliedman and Roth, in press).

Even if these problems cannot be resolved, thinking of political action as a public awareness resource can stretch our conceptions of what we must do to reshape public perception of people who are developmentally disabled. It can force us to look beyond the traditional tools of persuasive communication that we inherited from Madison Avenue. It can demonstrate that certain actions speak more eloquently and more directly than the most carefully written broadcast copy. Most important, it can continually remind us that to solve this critical yet complex problem, simple 60-second solutions do not seem to be the answer.

HOW WILL WE KNOW IF IT'S WORKING?

Senator: You are requesting $250,000 to mount a massive campaign to change the attitudes of citizens toward the developmentally disabled. Will you be able to come back next year and assure us that the money was well spent?

DD Director: Of course, Senator.

It is far easier to advise finding innovative solutions to public awareness problems than it is to implement them. Part of the reason for this is that program planners rarely have access to data that can tell them which of their past efforts worked and why, or, more likely, why not. Suppose that our mythical director comes back and says that the Council produced X number of public service announcements that ran Y number of times on Z stations; that the Council slide-tape program was presented A times before B different groups with a total audience of $C;$ that L brochures were mailed in sets of five to M households; and that the newsletter mailing list was expanded to $Q;$ that J workshops were conducted for K County Medical Societies; and that the hotline took 10,000 calls. The Senator may well agree that the money was well spent, but did the program work? Customarily, people tackle this question from three directions.

First, there are those who assume that if you produce something very carefully and expose it in the correct fashion to as many people as possible, a campaign will work. The material will communicate whatever message you put into it; people will listen to it and hear it; and finally, they will act on it. This is commonly known as the "hypodermic" approach to persuasive communication. The audience is viewed as a mass. The campaign is viewed as a "syringe" full of "information" which, when injected into the mass, will cause it to somehow change. People who follow this line of thinking are constantly striving to find the right kind of "syringes" and the right mixture of "information" to squirt out of it. Advertising agencies, for example, spend millions tinkering with the content and format of television spots and print materials, trying to strike the balance of medium and message that will reach people and move them.

Second, there are those who admit that simply injecting the right message directly into the mass through the right medium may not guarantee that people will hear you. There are "things" out there, the logic goes, that might distort what you're saying or dilute its impact. A message might run up against a brick wall of "customer" resistance, or it might run contrary to the prevailing wisdom of the community as expressed by its opinion leaders, or it might just get lost. People sensitive to these kinds of problems often undertake surveys to see if the message is getting through to people and doing its work.

Advertising agencies will survey the public to measure the rise and fall of "brand awareness," or "product recall."

Third, there are those who recognize that causing people to say one thing, rather than another, to an interviewer does not necessarily mean that you are also changing their behavior. People who "remember" a product called Era may continue to buy Tide. People who are "aware" of all the advantages of taking the train may still find the plane more convenient. Communicators sensitive to this gap between reported attitude changes and changes in behavior often try to find ways to measure changes in behavior and then link these changes to the campaign they have put together. Advertising agencies try to link "waves" of television spots with rises in sales, or they will interview purchasers of products to learn what "convinced" them to buy.

Where do DD Councils fit into this framework? All Councils recognize the need to evaluate what they are doing in public awareness. Most end up measuring performance through some combination of the first two techniques:

> "It's a great movie. We've distributed it to 400 groups this year. They all say they love it."
>
> "Those TV spots look as good as any Schlitz commercial I've seen. The station managers are bending over backwards to give us air play."
>
> "I really have problems with the way you underscore dependency in that spot. It's too reminiscent of the 'poster child' image."
>
> "We surveyed five classes before and after they read our materials. More than half showed more positive attitudes toward the developmentally disabled."
>
> "Sixty percent of the employers who came to our seminars reported that they left with a better understanding of how they could employ more disabled people."

These are traditionally valid measures of performance. Although they answer some questions, they do not necessarily answer the important one: Did the campaign produce more housing, better eduction, a wider range of jobs? Did it foster the growth of better transportation, better social services, a more receptive community? As any advertising executive will tell you, finding answers to *these* kinds of questions is a fearsome task. Many government agencies that undertake community education as part of their legislative mandate do not even try. When they do, their findings are often dismal. In 1974, M. S. Goodstadt reviewed the literature that reported on efforts to evaluate drug education. He found that, first:

> There is an almost total lack of evidence indicating beneficial effects of drug education. Very few educational programs have been evaluated and almost none have shown significant improvements in anything other than levels of knowledge; *attitudes and drug use have generally remained unaffected.* Second . . . there is very little scientific evidence from which one could

confidently draw conclusions regarding the effectiveness of drug education . . . it can only be concluded that the necessary evidence is not yet available, although the evidence that does exist is not encouraging (Goodstadt, 1974).

These were expensive lessons to learn. By the time these findings had been published, government and private organizations had been in the drug abuse business for more than 10 years. Millions of dollars had been spent while program planners struggled to find a way to measure what was happening at the bottom line, which in this case was incidence of drug use, not attitudes or awareness.

There is a moral buried here. It can be stated in two parts. First, DD Councils should *commit themselves to measuring* how well their public awareness programs work. Second, they should try to measure them in terms of *how they affect the bottom line*, how they help the Council achieve its primary mission of promoting more housing, a better protection and advocacy system, a more receptive community, and so on. Developing the capacity to do this will not only help Councils improve existing public awareness and education programs, but it will sensitize them to the wide range of forces operating in the community that affect the way people look at and behave toward developmentally disabled people. This alone can help Councils plan more carefully, more frugally, and come closer to nudging the bottom line.

REFERENCES

Ashmore, R.D. Background considerations in developing strategies for changing attitudes and behavior toward the mentally retarded. In M.J. Begab, *The Mentally Retarded and Society,* pp. 159–173. Baltimore: University Park Press, 1975.

Gliedman, J., and Roth, W. The grand illusion: Stigma, role expectation, and handicap.

Goodstadt, M.S. Myths and methodology in drug education: A critical review of the research on methods and programs of drug education. Unpublished paper. Addiction Research Foundation, Toronto, 1974.

Olsen, J.R. Primary prevention research: A preliminary review of program impact studies. Unpublished paper. Literature Search Task Group of the National Institute on Drug Abuse, 1976.

12
Vermont
"Project Awareness"

Toby Knox

Writing a chapter on the DD Council's citizen awareness activities in Vermont requires the same approach as does the planning of a citizen awareness program. A most important series of decisions must be made before pencil is put to paper or the first brochure is designed or PSA is written. Someone or some policy-making group must answer the questions: What is it we want to say, to whom, and why? In other words, goals must be established, and strategies to achieve those goals must be determined.

It would be useful first to define a few terms that are used in this chapter and should be a part of any citizen awareness effort.

A *goal* is a desired result. In the case of a citizen awareness program it may be a goal with a broad scope, such as increased public acceptance of persons with developmental disabilities, or a goal with a narrow scope, such as an informational campaign on the housing needs of the handicapped directed to a zoning board or a housing authority.

A *strategy* is the overall game plan devised to achieve the goal. There may be many ways to communicate a particular message. The reasons to select one approach or technique as opposed to another, or two approaches in tandem, must be based on an overall plan or strategy.

Often communicators confuse strategy and *techniques*, the methods or media used to present the message or information. We all like to see the finished product and are proud to present it to the Council as we did in school "show and tell." However, if the medium will not achieve or help to reach the goal, it should not be chosen.

The difficult part of this process comes before the brochure is written, the newsletter is printed, or the slides are photographed.

The questions that must be asked before any project is set in motion are: Why are we doing it? Will it help achieve our goal? How does it fit into the strategy? Time, effort, and money will be saved if these questions are answered as the first step of any citizen awareness project.

ESTABLISHING GOALS

The Vermont Developmental Disabilities Council established its "Project Awareness" in January, 1975. The need for the project stemmed from a Council perception that the general public and certain specific groups did not understand the needs, hopes, and desires of the developmentally disabled population.

In September, 1974, the Council developed a list of 10 barriers to service. Of the 10 barriers, 3 of them dealt in some way with the lack of citizen awareness. The barriers were described as follows:

1. "Consumers and professionals lack information regarding the existence of appropriate services and means of access to them."
2. "Lack of knowledge about developmental disabilities and community responsibility for developmental disabilities."
3. "Public fear and ignorance about developmentally disabled people."

These barriers have served as a guide and overall goals throughout the Project's existence.

VERMONT

Vermont is a small state with a population of under half a million. There are approximately 20,000 persons with one or more disability. As is the case in many states, the focus is starting to turn toward community living and more or better community-based service delivery systems. The 10 community mental health agencies that cover the state's 14 counties are developing into combined community mental health-developmental disabilities agencies and the four private citizens' advocacy groups are increasingly active throughout the state.

The DD Council receives the minimal federal allocation and thus does not have a large amount of money for the many areas requiring attention. While citizen awareness has been a high priority for the last 3 years, the budgets of Project Awareness have been modest, never reaching above $27,000 for a fiscal year. However, that the budget was never less than $18,000 reflects the Council's substantial commitment to citizen awareness.

DOING A LOT WITH A LITTLE

Following sound advertising and communications practices, one of the first strategies adopted was the decision to tie as many pieces of the project together as possible. In other words, to achieve the maximum impact for a small number of dollars spent we knew we would have to reinforce our message by coordinating the way we selected and utilized various communications techniques.

The second decision, mostly dictated by budget, was to undertake programs that would be inexpensive and yet would directly or indirectly reach the audience(s) desired.

A third important aspect of the planning was the resolve to take advantage of communications opportunities that were an intrinsic part of the Vermont life-style.

Toll-Free Telephone

One of the first, and most successful, programs initiated was a toll-free telephone line for consumers and others in search of assistance or information. The line, dubbed Dial Direct 4 Developmental Disabilities, or the "4D" line, is answered by the staff of the Community Mental Retardation Services Division of the Department of Mental Health. The purpose of the service is to provide information regarding the existence of appropriate services and to provide assistance in achieving access to them.

Numerous techniques were utilized to announce the line's existence and publicize the number. In addition to radio and television public service announcements and general press releases, a number of methods were tried that had small price tags and extensive visibility.

Following in the tradition of Alexander Graham Bell, the Council invited Vermont's governor to answer a prearranged first call from a Council member, calling from the other end of the state, to officially open the line. A short dedication ceremony was held, to which all consumer groups, community mental health agencies, state government service delivery agencies, members of the legislature, Vermont's Congressional delegation, and the press were invited. Favorable and widespread media coverage was given to the inauguration of the 4D line.

A discussion was held among members of the Council's Citizens Awareness Committee, the project's review board, on how to inform the group of Vermonters who might not read the newspapers, or watch much television, or listen to the radio about the existence of the line. Two methods were selected.

The first entailed having a poster designed and printed. The poster and a covering letter were sent to all of Vermont's town or city clerks with a special request. The first Tuesday in March is the traditional day Vermonters in all of he state's 246 organized towns and cities meet at the town or city hall to hold local elections, set town and school budgets and policy, and discuss town problems. It also is usually the only day in the year that townspeople get together in one location.

The request to the town clerks was to place the 4D line poster in a prominent location at the town hall. A telephone follow-up survey of town clerks after town meetings showed that many complied with the request.

The second publicity technique generated the broadest exposure to the line's number. Pitney Bowes' postage meter plates were made for the State government's six postal outlets. Every piece of mail metered by the State of Vermont for over 6 months advertised the Dial Direct line. This meant that every licensed motorist, every person receiving a tax form, every person on welfare and unemployment assistance, or anyone getting anything from the state received an envelope with the toll-free line number imprinted on it.

A third way that informed potential users of the line of its existence was having the poster reduced to a size that would fit into a business-size envelope. These miniposters, printed on a card stock, were stuffed in mailings and distributed to locations where they might be picked up, such as community mental health centers, state advocacy offices, state teacher's convention, and so on. One of the state's largest banks placed one in each bank statement. Unfortunately, a similar request made to the New England Telephone Company for stuffing a card in each bill was turned down.

Press Kit

No one disputes the power of the press as "gatekeepers" of information reaching the general public. It seems, however, that few people take the time to educate the press or give them the appropriate background information that is required for understanding an event or writing a story.

Because the term *developmental disabilities* was new to almost everyone and few seemed to know much about the disabilities, a press kit was organized and distributed to all press statewide. The contents consisted of some materials already in existence and some especially prepared.

The information pieces were:

Individual pamphlets on each disability written in lay terms, including specific sources for further information as well as the 4D line number
A similar pamphlet on developmental disabilities, the Council, and its mandate
A roster of Council members, including address and telephone if the local press desired a local contact
Information on the 4D line
A profile of Council activities and Council grants

A cover memo from the Council Chairperson explained the reason for the kit and invited requests for additional materials. While it was not anticipated that every kit would be read from cover to cover, the materials were assembled in a specially designed file folder for future study or reference.

Talk Shows

Numerous opportunities exist for free time on radio and television. Being a small state, however, Vermont has very few stations. However, being small makes it feasible to drive to any part of Vermont within several hours and hit all 20 radio stations with an interview or talk show. These shows have a high level of credibility with their audience and command faithful and loyal listeners.

Television interview shows in Vermont are not as plentiful as on radio. There are three in-state television stations and several that cover Vermont from neighboring states. On several occasions the Council Chairperson or the Commissioner of Mental Health appeared on television and discussed developmental disabilities. In keeping with our decision to tie all the pieces of the citizen awareness program together, on each radio and television show the 4D line was plugged and the informational pamphlets were offered to the audience.

Targeting the Message

While a large portion of the Project Awareness program was directed to the general public with hopes that it also would be of consequence to certain subgroups, specific messages were targeted to selected audiences. Narrowing the scope of the information to be transmitted to meet the interests of a group often can be the most fruitful part of an information and education project.

Too often the challenge offered to a citizen awareness program is to educate the public and change attitudes. While this is not an impossible task, it is a time-consuming, expensive, and, perhaps, frustrating experience. Transmitting small amounts of information to a certain public within the general public, however, can prove to be a worthwhile and rewarding endeavor.

Legislators Fact and Information File

The Vermont Council identified the members of the Vermont Legislature as being an audience that needed accurate and factual information on the subject of developmental disabilities. As with members of the press, state legislators are presumed to be experts on all subjects. Without staff and with limited research facilities available, legislators cannot hope to be aware of all the problems facing the state's residents and the government.

In an effort to assist legislators to become familiar with the needs, hopes, and desires of individuals with a disability and the problems they face, Project Awareness designed and assembled an introductory fact and information file. In keeping with the principle of making a little go a long way, many of the materials of the press kit were also designed with the legislators in mind. The materials were sent to members of the General Assembly at their home address before the legislative session commenced. A personally typed cover letter from the Council Chairperson invited requests for additional or more specific information.

A postcard survey of legislators taken by the Council at a later date showed that a majority of lawmakers appreciated the information and found it helpful.

The Council also has sponsored an annual luncheon for legislators during the legislative session to review the Council's legislative platform and give Council members and representatives and senators a chance to discuss mutual concerns. Building on these two foundation blocks, Project Awareness had a seminar for Council members to make them more effective in "influencing" legislation. The purpose was to educate Council members on the "ins" and "outs" of the legislative process, and while some of the information was old hat to more experienced Council members, the general consensus seemed to be that the time was well spent.

Technical Assistance

Several unsuccessful attempts by local organizations to open group homes in communities led the Council to take a long look at future state plans to develop intermediate care facilities for the developmentally disabled. As has been the case elsewhere, in several communities neighboring residents, homeowners, and the town zoning commissions reacted negatively to a proposal to establish a home for developmentally disabled adults.

In an attempt to avoid such reactions, confrontations, and negative public debate, Project Awareness offered technical citizen awareness assistance to the state's community mental health agencies who were planning to site, place, and operate ICF/DDs. The program was divided into five phases. The first phase called for a study of successful and unsuccessful community-based residence siting and placement efforts and to determine what the plans and needs of community mental health agencies were. Phase two called for the preparation of a model citizen awareness strategy and plan. Phases three and four were to review the model strategy with groups planning the development of housing and adapt the strategy and plan to local needs. The last phase was to serve as a technical consultant to groups with needs in the citizen awareness area.

Due to difficulties at other levels in obtaining the funds and contracts, the development of ICF/DDs did not occur as planned. The one community mental health agency that started the process and received assistance from Project Awareness later voted not to have an ICF/DD and ceased its efforts.

The idea, however, of providing citizen awareness assistance or consultation to organizations like community mental health agencies is a valid one. We are all aware of the unhappy and unfortunate situations that may occur when group homes are suggested for a neighborhood. Often this is the case when the persons sponsoring the home do not plan ahead and take sound public relations steps to offset, negate, or minimize any opposition. This is an example of where targeting a message to a specific group or groups really can pay off.

The examples given here are a few of the activities undertaken by the Vermont Developmental Disabilities Council's Project Awareness during a 3-year period. If anything has been learned throughout this period it is that the campaign for the hearts and minds of our audience(s) is never ending. With consumers being deluged with 1,800 to 2,500 advertising messages a day, the competition for being remembered is stiff. With General Motors, Coca-Cola, and General Foods spending millions of dollars a year to sell their products or to keep them in front of the consuming public, a few public service announcements, brochures, newsletters, and slide/tapes seem like a lean arsenal with which to offset ignorance, abate fear, and help to persuade the public that persons with disabilities have needs, hopes, and desires similar to all citizens.

It may sound like an insurmountable task, but it can be done. Changing or formulating public opinions and attitudes demands commitment and patience. A constant vigil should be kept for positive citizen awareness opportunities, and the attention of the public must not be allowed to shift when issues demand action.

Philadelphia department store executive John Wanamaker has been quoted as saying he never knew which half of his advertising budget was being spent in a beneficial manner and which half was being wasted. He did know, however, that he could not stop advertising.

Developmental Disabilities Councils cannot always put their fingers on the rate of attitude change or opinion formulation toward their state's disabled population. When it comes to budget preparation time, the lack of a clear evaluation can often be frustrating and could possibly mean the shifting of dollars and commitment to other projects.

Do not let this happen. DD Councils must continue to support citizen awareness projects and keep the concerns and goals of individuals with disabilities before the public. Citizen awareness is another term for communications, and only by communicating openly, often, and effectively will the needs of persons with developmental disabilities be recognized.

Part IV
SERVICES

Part IV includes six chapters, which explore additional key aspects of the DD movement. Each makes its own contribution to further defining the nature of the DD movement.

Chapter 12, "Human Services Ecology," is another updated excerpt from *The Orientation Notebook* by Paula Breen and Gary Richman. In it they discuss the concept of comprehensive services for people who are developmentally disabled. Legislative intent is articulated through several key dimensions of a comprehensive service network.

"Deinstitutionalization Procedures," by G. Ronald Neufeld, provides an elaboration of another important construct inherent in the DD movement. Neufeld cites and discusses the main principles, objectives, and activities that can be subsumed under the rubric of deinstitutionalization.

About one-third of our nation's population lives in rural areas. Rural areas differ greatly from urban and suburban areas in ways that affect service delivery to the developmentally disabled. Charles Horejsi, in "Service Delivery in Rural Areas," presents some of the problems involved in rural service delivery. He also points out a number of positive implications derived from strengths common to rural communities.

In "Role of the Consumer in Planning and Delivering Services," Frank Warren discusses several of the different roles that consumers can play as well as the issues related to these roles. His remarks serve as a challenge to productive integration of differing sources of DD Council effort.

Ronald Wiegerink, Vince Parrish, and Iris Buhl, in "Consumer Involvement in Human Services," provide further elaboration on the theme of consumerism. After citing a number of reasons for involving consumers in the service delivery process, they describe the Regional Intervention Program, a highly successful effort that included parents in managing and delivering services.

The concluding chapter is "Future of Service Delivery Systems for Handicapped Individuals" by Donald J. Stedman and Ronald Wiegerink. It provides a critical review of current issues in the field of services for handicapped people. Stedman and Wiegerink conclude their chapter with a series of recommendations to increase the effectiveness of the service delivery system.

13

The Human
Services Ecology

Paula Breen and Gary Richman

The 1970 DD act (PL 94-103) required that each state develop a *"state plan
for the provision of services . . . for persons with developmental disabilities."*

The original law defined "services for developmentally disabled persons" as follows:

> The term "services for persons with developmental disabilities" means
> specialized services or special adaptations of generic services directed toward the alleviation of a developmental disability or toward the social,
> personal, physical, or economic habilitation or rehabilitation of an individual
> with such a disability.

The text continues the definition by listing 16 services:

> and such terms include diagnosis, evaluation, treatment, personal care, day
> care, domiciliary care, special living arrangements, training, education,
> sheltered employment, recreation, counseling of the individual with such a
> disability and of his family, protective and other social and socio-legal
> services, information and referral services, follow-along services, and transportation services necessary to assure delivery of services to persons with
> developmental disabilities.

It is important to grasp the legislative intent of this definition and listing. Two
points should be emphasized:

1. This "laundry list" of services was intended to be comprehensive and
    inclusive, not finite and exclusive. Drafters of the legislation chose terms
    that were general enough, loose enough, to cover any kind of program a
    developmentally disabled person might need or want. In early orientation
    conferences on developmental disabilities, the Developmental Disabilities Office staff challenged the audiences to think of some service or
    activity that could not be covered under 1 of the 16 rubrics. Even the most

exotic services could perhaps be funded as "recreation services" or "special living arrangements."
2. The 16 services were not meant to be discrete entities or independent activities. Transportation has no value in and of itself; developmental disabilities transportation services must be linked with some service or program destination. Developmental disabilities diagnostic services cannot stand alone, but must be a part of a service configuration for the individual and his family that includes evaluation, treatment, counseling, and other supportive services.

The developmental disabilities service concept is marked by emphasis on comprehensive, coordinated, life-long, supportive services for the disabled individual and his family. This emphasis is unique among all other federal human service legislation, which defines services for a particular phase of life or age limits (i.e., special education: 3-21 years, or vocational rehabilitation: the employment years); or provides for limited kinds of services (i.e., Title XX: social services, but not medical or educational services).

The reference in the definition to generic services reflects another characteristic of the developmental disabilities service concept: its emphasis on "normalization," the appropriateness and right of handicapped individuals to have access to services from community agencies serving the general public.

In the 1975 developmental disabilities act Congress demonstrated an additional interest in directing the developmental disabilities program's attention to specific unserved and underserved clients and matching them with appropriate services. The 1975 law used the State Plan to direct Councils to key groups and services within the developmental disabilities service concept:

KEY TARGET GROUPS	SERVICES
Infants	Early screening
Preschool children	Maternal care
Multiply handicapped children	Home care
	Infant stimulation
	Parent counseling
Adults	Counseling
Economically disadvantaged persons	Program coordination
	Follow-along
	Protective services
	Personal advocacy

Given the definition, listing of services, and values embodied in the developmental disabilities service concept, how can states act to make services for the developmentally disabled a reality in communities? Clearly, the 1975 law did not provide sufficient funds to support comprehensive developmental disabilities services. However, the act did suggest a *resource strategy* for developmental disabilities. First, the law called for utilization of "generic services." Second, it required state Developmental Disabilities Councils to:

> Describe (A) the quality, extent, and scope of services being provided, or to be provided, to persons with developmental disabilities under such other State plans for Federally assisted State programs as may be specified by the Secretary, but in any case including education for the handicapped, vocational rehabilitation, public assistance, medical assistance, social services, maternal and child health, crippled children's services, and comprehensive health and mental health plans, and (B) how funds allotted to the State in accordance with section 132 [the state formula grant] will be used to complement and augment rather than duplicate or replace services and facilities for persons with developmental disabilities which are eligible for Federal assistance under such other State programs.

The impact of that provision was to charge state Developmental Disabilities Councils with a responsibility to influence other federal-state programs to comply with existing constitutional and statutory mandates; this may involve cooperative planning and program innovations. The provision implied that Councils would direct their actions toward asserting the rights to service for people with developmental disabilities under other federal-state programs.

The text of the 1975 developmental disabilities law elaborated on this resource strategy and made more explicit what the original language had implied. The 1975 legislation required states, as part of their State Plan for the provision of services, to utilize as much as possible the resources and personnel in existing related community programs and to assure appropriate supplemental health, educational, or social services for persons with developmental disabilities. The State Plan also was to provide for the maximum utilization of all volunteers serving under the Domestic Volunteer Service Act of 1973 (PL 93-113) and other appropriate voluntary organizations. To fully facilitate coordinated service planning and to have a more direct influence on other federal-state programs, the Council was authorized by the law to have prior review and comment, to the maximum extent feasible, on all State Plans that relate to programs affecting persons with developmental disabilities. This included: Title XX Social Services, Title XIX Medicaid, Title V Material and Child Health, and the federal-state plans for housing, transportation, comprehensive employment and training (CETA), and others.

The developmental disabilities legislation of 1975 also contained a significant statement of Congressional findings concerning service rights of developmentally disabled people. Although the findings carried no authorization of funds or sanctions for enforcement or implementation, the statement provided a potentially important precedent and clarification of Congressional intent regarding the use of public funds. A portion of the law is reprinted here:

RIGHTS OF THE DEVELOPMENTALLY DISABLED

Congress makes the following findings respecting the rights of persons with developmental disabilities:

1) Persons with developmental disabilities have a right to appropriate treatment, services, and habilitation for such disabilities.

2) The treatment, services, and habilitation for a person with developmental disabilities should be designed to maximize the developmental potential of the person and should be provided in the setting that is least restrictive of the person's personal liberty.

3) The Federal government and the States both have an obligation to assure that public funds are not provided to any institutional or other residential program for persons with developmental disabilities that—

    a) does not provide treatment, services, and habilitation which is appropriate to the needs of such persons; or

    b) does not meet . . . minimum standards

The law listed six minimum standards regarding diet, medical and dental services, use of restraints, visiting hours, and compliance with fire and safety codes. The intent of Congress is clarified by the following excerpts from the conference report:

These rights are generally included in the conference substitute in recognition by the conferees that the developmentally disabled, particularly those who have the misfortune to require institutionalization, have a right to receive appropriate treatment for the conditions for which they are institutionalized, and that this right should be protected and assured by the Congress and the courts.

and

The conference committee recognizes that the six minimum standards are designed to protect the basic human needs of developmentally disabled individuals and will not in themselves ensure quality habilitation and adequate treatment programs. The committee therefore does not intend these standards to preempt or supplant any existing Federal or State standards currently in force (e.g. standards applicable to Intermediate Care Facilities for the Mentally Retarded under Medicaid), which may require more detailed or higher standards of care.

To implement the Congressional intent the 1975 law mandated responsibilities for the Secretary of HEW and for the Developmental Disabilities Councils. The Secretary was directed to conduct a study of federal standards and regulations impacting the quality of services for the developmentally disabled under vocational rehabilitation, special education, Medicare, Medicaid, and social services.

To assist states in protecting an individual's rights to quality services appropriate for his needs the law included three interrelated mechanisms:

Individualized habilitation plan
Evaluation system
Advocacy and protective service

The Individual Habilitation Plan (IHP) is a written agreement between a disabled person and a service provider. The plan sets forth a prescription for programming action tailored to the individual's needs. It defines the mutual goals and objectives of the services program, the barriers to achieving those goals, and the means to attain the goals. The IHP states how multiple services will be coordinated and names the individual who will be responsible for implementing and coordinating the service plan.

Technically, the developmental disabilities law only requires an IHP for persons with developmental disabilities receiving services funded in part by Developmental Disabilities Council funds. However, the IHP concept, that of requiring service agencies to specify in writing how programs will be tailored to meet individual needs, is included in several major federal programs, including the Vocational Rehabilitation Act, Title XX Social Services, and the SSI Child Referral Program. Ideally, the format and procedures developed by the Developmental Disabilities Council for individual habilitation plans for developmental disabilities should be utilized for developmentally disabled people in these and other human service programs.

Requirements for written prescriptive plans reflect growing concerns of policy makers and society as a whole for accountability mechanisms, quality assurance, and evaluation of program performance and resource allocation decisions. This broad commitment to more adequately evaluate the returns on our investments in human services is found in the 1975 developmental disabilities law's provisions for an evaluation system. Just as the IHP focuses attention of providers on the individual to be served, the evaluation system is intended to measure agency performance on the basis of progress made by individuals receiving agency services. The requirements for an evaluation system set forth in the 1975 law reflect Congressional concern for the lack of adequate methods to evaluate services and service systems in a way that truly reflects the impact of such services in meeting the needs of the developmentally disabled. The Senate report noted that too often evaluation of human services programs has degenerated to a "numbers racket" in which mere numbers were used to replace the individual benefit or progress as the criteria of success.

By April, 1978, states were to be committed to a time-phased plan for the implementation of an evaluation system compatible with the model developed by HEW. Systems were to provide for objective measures of client progress (using data from IHPs) and a method for evaluating programs providing services for developmental disabilities clients. Confidentiality of individual files must be protected. The system is to be in use in the states by October, 1979. At HEW request, the time lines have been revised forward 1 year, with the initial system due in April, 1979.

It is important to see the relationship between the provisions for individual habilitation plans and the required evaluation system. In the words of the Senate report on the Senate's version of the 1975 developmental diabilities bill (S462), the individual habilitation plan is intended to serve as "a tool not only for the development of [the] individual, but also as a means of evaluating the quality and performance of the program and is a necessary component if appropriate agencies are going to evaluate the system to see if it is providing a desirable outcome for the individual within that system." Thus the IHP is a key data source for the evaluation system.

The third component of this tripartite mechanism for protecting individual rights is the Advocacy and Protective Service System. Such a system has been in operation in every state since October, 1977. Funds were allocated to states on the formula basis to assist in developing a system independent of any state agency providing services. The advocacy system is charged with responsibility to ensure protection of the rights of the developmentally disabled and authorized to pursue appropriate legal, administrative, or other remedies. According to the Senate report this independent agency is needed to:

> provide a mechanism by which a developmentally disabled individual within the delivery system has the means to reach outside of the established delivery system for examination of situations in which his rights as an individual citizen may be violated.

This third component also focuses on the individual and is designed to assure the delivery of *appropriate, high quality* services for all developmentally disabled persons.

The 1978 developmental disabilities legislation reinforces the three rights and quality assurance mechanisms, but it makes a significant change in the overall DD resource strategy. While much of the language regarding the 16 service areas and the use of generic services survives in the 1978 act, it offers a new thrust. In addition to the 16 comprehensive all-inclusive services that were to get special attention from DD Councils in their planning and advocacy activities, the 1978 act intends for DD Councils to use at least 65% of the formula grant to directly fund services in any two of the four "priority services." The four priority services are defined in the act as:

1. Case management services: "services to persons with developmental disabilities as will assist them in gaining access to needed social, medical, educational and other services." The term includes "follow-along services which ensure, through a continuing relationship, life-long if

necessary, between an agency or provider and a person with a developmental disability and the person's immediate relatives or guardians, that the changing needs of the person and the family are recognized and appropriately met''; as well as ''coordination services which provide to persons with developmental disabilities support, access to (and coordination of) other services, information on programs and services, and monitoring of the person's progress.''

2. Child development services: services to ''assist in the prevention, identification and alleviation of developmental disabilities in children.'' The term includes early intervention services, counseling and training of parents, early identification diagnosis, and evaluation of developmental disabilities.

3. Alternative community living arrangement services: services to ''assist persons with developmental disabilities in maintaining suitable residential arrangements in the community, and includes in-house services (such as personal aides and attendants and other domestic assistance and supportive services), family support services, foster care services, group living services, respite care, and staff training, placement, and maintenance services.''

4. Nonvocational social-developmental services: services to ''assist persons with developmental disabilities in performing daily living and work activities.''

14

Deinstitutionalization Procedures

G. Ronald Neufeld

BACKGROUND

A great deal of controversy has been aroused over the concept of deinstitutionalization in America. Along with the controversial nature of the concept and its underlying values, there is widespread disagreement surrounding the use of the term *deinstitutionalization* and how it is defined. The creation of a semantic argument over the definition of a term is often an indirect way of attacking basic constructs and values. Many persons who insist upon arguing about a definition of deinstitutionalization seem to be threatened by the activities associated with the term. They are unable to attack the underlying values, beliefs, and constructs of deinstitutionalization directly and so they participate in unproductive arguments over definition.

The basic construct or armature for the deinstitutionalization movement concerns the normalizing of environments for disabled citizens. This includes: 1) the creation and maintenance of environments that do not impose excessive restrictions upon disabled persons, 2) the creation of arrangements that bring persons as close as possible to the social and cultural mainstream, and 3) guarantees that the human and legal rights of disabled citizens are protected. Within the framework of these constructs a wide variety of activities and programs should be carried on, ranging from institutional reform procedures, to institutional depopulation programs, to designs aimed at creating comprehensive community programs for disabled people.

It is estimated that 200,000 persons are residents in large public facilities in America. Some of the negative characteristics associated with these institutions are regimentation, lack of privacy, impersonal treatment, limited freedom and independence for the residents, and limited interaction between the residents and the "outside" world (Kugel & Wolfensberger, 1969). The larger the institution and the larger the geographical area that it must serve, the more difficult it is to normalize that environment for its residents. Activities aimed at improving conditions for residents in institutions can legitimately be called deinstitutionalization. As long as our society allows the placement of citizens in large residential facilities, we have an obligation to do our utmost to normalize those environments. The application of standards and the monitoring of activities by advocates are among the institutional procedures that are being employed in an attempt to renew institutional programs and counteract the negative characteristics often associated with large residential facilities.

Although activity aimed at the renewal of institutions is certainly a legitimate deinstitutional concern, this chapter focuses upon deinstitutionalization as activity aimed at depopulating institutions and creating services in communities as alternatives to institutional placement. Obviously, there is no single approach to accomplishing the depopulation and community service objectives of deinstitutionalization. The purpose of this chapter is to present a series of activities and guidelines that are sufficiently specific for an organization or a group of people to develop a plan for action.

There are several different geographical levels at which initiatives could be undertaken to develop deinstitutionalization plans. The levels include organizations from local communities, multicounty regions, or state-level units. There are many dormant state and regional plans in file drawers across this country (Paul, Wiegerink, & Thiele, 1975). The litmus test of any deinstitutionalization activity as it is defined for this chapter concerns the number of disabled citizens adequately served in community programs and the number of institutionalized residents that are brought home. Utilizing these criteria, state and regional designs have been largely unsuccessful. The difficulty factor in accomplishing deinstitutionalization activity increases at each level from local to state settings. Although the procedures suggested herein can be put together at any level, decentralization is suggested in order to place substantial responsibility in the hands of local units. At the same time, roles and responsibilities are suggested for organizations at each level.

DECENTRALIZING SERVICE DELIVERY

The first principle in a deinstitutionalization design is to decentralize service provision. In this connection, the first objective is to create small geographical and population areas (Neufeld, 1977). A population base of approximately 100,000 persons should be considered. In rural areas, it is helpful if the population and geographical unit corresponds to a local political unit, such as county government. A population base of 100,000 persons is small enough to obtain client needs assessment information, identify and monitor existing resources, and yet provide an array of services for disabled citizens. In very sparsely populated areas, it is possible that two or three counties may need to be combined to form a service area. However, distance is an important factor and residents should be protected from having to travel long distances for service. Wherever possible, the principle of delivering service to the client should be observed, not delivering the client to the service. An additional advantage to establishing small geographical and population units is that an organization at this level is likely to have fewer vested interests to coordinate, communication is less complicated, and the commitments of and assistance from local citizens is less difficult to recruit. Federal and state resources for disabled persons should be deployed directly into these catchment areas. Only limited resources should be retained for administrative, monitoring, and technical assistance functions at the state level.

ESTABLISHING LOCAL HUMAN SERVICE AREAS

In order to accomplish the objectives of deinstitutionalization, it is often necessary to adjust the priorities of a state bureaucracy and redirect the flow of resources (Paul, Wiegerink, & Neufeld, 1975). Objective number two is to establish local human service boards. It is desirable to have a legislative base for these boards and they should be authorized to receive money and operate programs. At least 50% of the board membership should be consumers or consumer representatives. Beyond that, there should be representatives from a variety of interest groups, including different consumer organizations, different agencies, and different professional entities. Activities would include:

1. Client needs assessment
2. Identification of program resources
3. Service coordination
4. Service development
5. Policy development for service delivery

In connection with service delivery, the local boards should not ignore the value of contracting for service to private organizations. It is suggested that the local human service boards should view themselves as the single human service advisory mechanism to the local political units. If more than one county political unit is encompassed by this board, then the county governmental units should be invited to place representatives on the board. A close connection with local governments would enable the board to sensitize local politicians to needs in the human service area, enable these organizations to participate in decision making, and thereby increase the probability of obtaining a fair share of the financial resources that are available to local governments.

CONSIDERATIONS IN DEVELOPING
A UNIFIED COMMUNITY HUMAN SERVICE SYSTEM

Adversaries of institutions often propose the immediate depopulation and dismantling of institutions. The depopulation and dismantling of institutions for disabled persons will not occur until stable, comprehensive community services are in place (Lafave, et al., 1968). Objective number three, therefore, is for the local human service board to provide total care for disabled citizens in their catchment area. When a comprehensive service network has been established, only disabled persons with highly specialized needs would be sent out of their catchment area.

One simple way to organize community services is to develop services around day, evening, and night modules. These three modules might be viewed as priorities one, two, and three in the order listed as resources are identified to develop new and needed programs. Day programs would feature education and training and employment. Evening modules would feature social and recreation activities, and the night module would offer lodging on short- and long-term bases. Respite care should be available to natural and foster families at all times. An important principle to keep in mind when planning for residential service is to encourage parents to keep their children at home whenever possible until they reach adulthood. Perhaps the most difficult and sensitive consideration for community services concerns residential alternatives for children and youth without suitable family resources and for disabled adults who need to be separated from their parents. The normalization concept would suggest that we should create family-like environments. In present-day America, it is unusual to find more than five or six persons in a single dwelling. An attempt should be made whenever possible to create residential resources that replicate natural family conditions.

This community service arrangement should be operated by a small administrative unit that is directly accountable to the human service board. The human service board in turn would establish policy for the governance of the overall programs. Again, it should be pointed out that contracts for service with private organizations should be considered as community services are developed.

The first sign of a successful community program is that total care is being provided locally and no one is being committed to an institution (Lafave, 1974). A major deterrent to the deinstitutionalization movement is parents with children in institutions. They fear that community programs are unstable and that if their children are placed in a community facility, the community program may close, their child will be returned to their home, and they will be left with no support. It is likely that this source of resistance to the deinstitutionalization movement would vanish if parents had reasonable assurance that community programs were stable. Also, the depopulation activities of institutions will proceed with much less difficulty when community services are in place.

INSTITUTIONAL DEPOPULATION PROCEDURES

In recent years there has been a dramatic increase in the cost of operating and maintaining large institutions. In spite of the huge sums of money that are currently being spent on institutions, many are unable to pass even minimum standards. A number of facilities that the courts have examined have been adjudicated unconstitutional for failing to provide even minimal care for their residents. It is estimated that almost 200,000 persons are still housed in the large residential facilities where the majority of our public resources for disabled citizens are spent. At the same time, it has been estimated that less than 5% of our handicapped citizens are served in these programs. The combination of high cost for care, substandard conditions in institutions, and the small proportion of disabled persons served in institutions leads a growing number of concerned citizens to question the present use of institutions (Stewart, et al., 1968).

When community services are in place and admissions to institutions are curtailed, depopulation procedures can be considered. Objective number four in our deinstitutionalization design is for community service boards to bring all citizens from their catchment area back home. Again, it is suggested that a local community should not wait for action by the state agency or a regional institution. The local human service board should exercise its own initiatives. In the first place, the community human service board should utilize a regional facility only for highly specialized medical service. Rigid criteria for admission to this service should be established and a single screening mechanism at the local level should carefully examine each placement recommendation.

In order to accomplish the depopulation objective, it is suggested that resident placement teams from each service area be organized. These teams should consist of three to four members with skills in identifying the medical treatment and training needs of residents and knowledge of community resources. These teams would begin by locating all of the citizens from their catchment areas who are located in institutions. They would then visit those residents to determine their needs, and then attempt to locate appropriate existing services or create new services in order to bring their citizens home. It is anticipated that residents with fewer handicapping conditions would be the first to be placed. As this occurred, staff-to-resident ratios would increase, thus strengthening the capability of the institution to conduct more intense and improved treatment and training procedures for the more severely handicapped citizens (Lafave, et al., 1966).

It should be pointed out that all of the objectives proposed thus far can be planned and coordinated by a state or regional organization in cooperation with local units. Furthermore, the activities could be conducted in cooperation with one local unit or many local units simultaneously. If, however, state or regional organizations are not moving in the direction of these objectives, a local unit is encouraged to act independently to achieve each of the stated objectives.

The objectives listed from this point forward focus upon the roles and functions of regional and state organizations as backup mechanisms to the local units. Strong support from state and regional bodies would certainly expedite the attainment of deinstitutionalization goals and objectives, but it is not essential, and local communities should not wait for their leadership.

A ROLE FOR REGIONAL FACILITIES

If institutions are to be emptied of all inappropriate placements and if community programs are to be developed to replace them, several additional forces will have to be dealt with. These forces include threatened employees in institutions, the unions that represent these employees, communities that rely on economic support from institutions, and public attitudes that fear the integration of disabled persons into the social mainstream (Lafave, et al., 1967). Two deinstitutionalization objectives are outlined below that deal with these forces and are antagonistic to the deinstitutionalization movement. At the same time, they indicate the role that a regional facility can play in deinstitutionalization.

Deinstitutionalization objective number five is to develop a technical assistance and training program at the regional level. Surplus staff from the decreasing number of institutionalized residents would be the first to enroll in a training program. They should be trained for positions in community programs. At the same time, a regional training resource should be ongoing in order to provide high quality preservice and inservice training for community program staff. In addition to the training resource, it is suggested that the regional program be prepared to provide responsive, on-site technical assistance to both the local boards and the service providers at the local level. Technical assistance and training would be offered in areas like program planning and evaluation, program development and service delivery, resource development, and public awareness programs.

Deinstitutionalization objective number six is to prepare the regional facility to provide only highly specialized medical treatment for disabled citizens: treatment that is likely to be unavailable in many small communities. In this connection strict admissions criteria should be established to prevent communities from making inappropriate referrals.

THE ROLE AND FUNCTION OF A STATE AGENCY

It has already been pointed out that state agencies have demonstrated limited success in accomplishing deinstitutional objectives. This chapter proposes the decentralization of power and resources and suggests that deinstitutionalization initiatives be placed in the hands of local human service boards. In this design, state agencies would be withdrawn from the service provider role and placed in a political and administrative enabling role. To a large extent, financial resources would simply flow through the state agency to the local human service boards.

Although a local human service board could conceivably attain the foregoing deinstitutionalization goals, an alliance among local, regional, and state organizations is recommended. The following objectives describe the role and function of a state agency in a deinstitutionalization design.

Deinstitutionalization objective number seven proposes that state agencies provide administrative and political support for the local human service boards. First, they would help the boards obtain fiscal resources. Second, they would establish standards for local programs and monitor the services needed.

Deinstitutionalization objective number eight proposes that state agencies provide resources for the regional medical facility and provide technical assistance to the regional facility concerning available state and federal resources.

Deinstitutionalization objective number nine proposes that state agencies function as a human service research arm of the legislature. In response to local and regional directives, the state agency would analyze existing human service legislation and propose new legislation.

Deinstitutionalization objective number 10 proposes that the state agency, through public hearings and public awareness campaigns, would be responsible for conducting extensive public education campaigns aimed at expanding the tolerance boundaries of the public for accepting disabled citizens.

Finally, it is suggested that state agencies should take steps to establish advisory boards with consumer representatives from different regions throughout the state.

EXPERIMENTS IN DEINSTITUTIONALIZATION

In the past decade, a number of states have attempted to develop and implement deinstitutionalization plans. Success stories are limited, and the author is not aware of any state that has pulled together all of the pieces of the foregoing design. However, portions of this design have been attempted in different parts of the country. Several of these examples are presented next.

First, one possible reason for the failure of many deinstitutionalization activities is that they have been organized within geographical and population units that are too large. A case can be constructed for keeping service delivery units small.

DEINSTITUTIONALIZATION IN JEFFERSON COUNTY

Jefferson County is a rural county in New York that includes a total population of 100,000 citizens. Twelve years ago, Jefferson County had one public school-sponsored class for retarded persons. The only choice for most families with retarded members was to keep their children at home where there were no community services or send them away to a state institution. Dissatisfied with their limited options, the parents organized to establish their own alternative system of education for their children, who were denied public education. They had three goals in mind: 1) to provide educational opportunities for their children, 2) to prove to public schools that their children could benefit from training, and 3) to obtain support from public schools in the process of providing education and training for their children. At present, services for retarded citizens include diagnostic medical evaluations, full-time infant care, sheltered employment, hospitals, and supervised independent living. With the advent of mandatory education legislation in the state of New York, the Jefferson County school system assumed responsibility for the education and training programs that the parent organization was running, and the parent organization is using its resources to develop additional services. A small amount of federal money was obtained to help Jefferson County bring their institutionalized citizens back home. In order to accomplish this objective, a diagnostic team was organized consisting of a full-time social worker and part-time consultants from psychiatry, medicine, vocational rehabilitation, and education. The teams' activities were to: 1) identify all Jefferson County residents in state schools, 2) evaluate each resident's disability and potential for community placement, 3) arrange for placement in appropriate community programs, 4) continue efforts to prevent admissions to state institutions, 5) evaluate the impact of community placement upon former residents of state schools, and 6) develop a procedure that may serve as a model to other rural communities.

The Jefferson County program demonstrates several of these principles. First, strong initiatives were taken by a local body. Second, the population base is small, thereby simplifying needs assessment resources identification and service coordination. Finally, they established a diagnostic team to bring their institutionalized residents back home. Two years ago, community programs in Jefferson County were serving approximately 500 citizens each day. Services included education and training programs during the day, respite care, and nighttime recreation. For residents unable to return to their natural homes, over 100 family care living arrangements were created. If present estimates of disability incidence are accurate, there are still disabled citizens in their county not receiving needed service, indicating that additional resources are needed. Nevertheless, the Jefferson County program is exemplary. The model could be incorporated into a larger regional or state design. The Jefferson County activity provides us with an example of a single community that has taken the initiative to develop its own deinstitutionalization program with limited external support.

COMMUNITY BOARDS IN WASHINGTON STATE

Washington is an example of a state that established a network of community boards. They were established by legislation and are authorized to receive funds and operate programs in their catchment areas. It is also an example of a state that established a network of privately owned group homes under contracts for service. The Washington plan proposes to establish sufficient group homes across the state to stabilize their total institutional population at 2,360 in 1980.

The weakness of the Washington design concerns the lack of coordination among community boards, their regional mechanisms, and their existing state institutions. Likewise, the community boards cover too large a geographical area and too large a population base. The design in Washington provides us with community service boards established by legislation and contracts for service to private organizations.

DEINSTITUTIONALIZATION AND PUBLIC SCHOOLS

There are very few examples of deinstitutionalization activity that indicate coordination with public schools. The deinstitutionalization activity that is operating in Jefferson County is an exception. In this county a local parent organization launched several demonstration programs. Having demonstrated the effectiveness of training for disabled persons and with the advent of mandatory education legislation, the demonstration programs were incorporated into the public school program.

In Madison, Wisconsin, there is an example of a school system that has taken the initiative to deinstitutionalize its catchment area. Services provided by the school system are directed toward all ages, from birth to adulthood, and extend to all ability levels. It is reported that no preschool or school-age persons have been placed in residential institutions for more than 4 years because of the services provided by the school system.

Agency coordination of programs and resources at all levels—local, regional, state, and national—has always been a problem. Public schools everywhere need to examine their role in providing education and training for severely and profoundly disabled citizens. The creation of mandatory education legislation is a great step in this direction. Now we need to find more examples of areas in which this legislation is being successfully implemented and make sure that there is coordination of this activity at the local level along with consumer involvement.

CONCLUSION

A growing number of citizens and parents of disabled children believe that the principles of normalization and least restrictive alternatives for disabled persons are often violated in institutions. They long for the day when some ancient alchemy will abolish these dehumanizing environments and create a new, trouble-free world for this minority population, whose cries are seldom heard in the stream of political and bureaucratic activity. It is time we realized that the only alchemy for deinstitutionalization is the chemistry between concerned citizens that prompts them to organize around their mutual interests to normalize environments for disabled citizens. This chapter has outlined a plan to help concerned citizens for deinstitutionalization.

First, it is suggested that strong initiatives should be placed in the hands of local communities. Second, small geographical service areas should be identified containing a relatively small population base. Third, community human service boards with legislative authority to receive funds and operate programs should be established. To the extent possible, these boards should be attached to local political units. Fourth, only highly specialized medical treatment facilities should exist at a regional, multicounty level. Fifth, local human service boards and local providers should have backup support in the form of training and technical assistance from regional facilities and from the state agencies. Finally, we should recognize that community programs should be developed in order to stabilize the population in institutions. After this has been accomplished, then institutional depopulation procedures can be launched. The major deinstitutional objectives discussed in this chapter are listed below.

A. Local Human Service Boards
    1. To create small geographical and population areas
    2. To establish local human service boards in each of the geographical areas
    3. To provide total care for disabled citizens in small geographical catchment areas
    4. To bring all institutionalized residents home to their geographical catchment area

B. Regional Facilities
    1. To develop a regional technical assistance and training facility
    2. To develop a regional medical facility to provide highly specialized medical care and treatment

C. State Agency Activity
    1. To provide administrative and political support to local human service boards
    2. To provide administrative and political support to the regional facility
    3. To function as a human service research arm of the legislature
    4. To develop statewide public education programs concerning the rights and needs of disabled citizens

REFERENCES

Kugel, R. B., and Wolfensberger, W. Changing patterns in residential services for the mentally retarded. Washington, D.C.: President's Committee on Mental Retardation, 1969.

Lafave, H. G. What is a model community-based service system? Paper presented before the Massachusetts Association for the Advancement of Human Services, Boston, December, 1974.

Lafave, H. G., Stewart, A., and Grunberg, F. Community care of the mentally ill: Implication of the Saskatchewan Plan. *Community Mental Health Journal*, 1968, *4(1)*, 37–45.

Lafave, H. G., Stewart, A. R., Grunberg, F., and Mackinnon, A. A. The Weyburn Experience: Reducing intake as a factor in phasing out a large mental hospital. *Comprehensive Psychiatry*, 1967, *8(4)*, 239–248.

Lafave, H. G., Stewart, A., Grunberg, F., and March, N. Reducing admissions and increasing discharges in Saskatchewan Hospital. *Canada's Mental Health*, 1966, January-February.

Neufeld, G. R. Deinstitutionalization: An examination of approaches. In J. L. Paul, D. J. Stedman, and G. R. Neufeld (Eds.), *Deinstitutionalization: Implications for Policy and Program Development*. 1977.

Paul, J. L., Wiegerink, R., and Neufeld, G. R. Deinstitutionalization and advocacy planning for the developmentally disabled: Conference design and rationale. In J. L. Paul, R. Wiegerink, and G. R. Neufeld (Eds.), *Advocacy: A Role for DD Councils*. Chapel Hill, N.C.: DDTAS, 1975.

Paul, J. L., Wiegerink, R., and Thiele, R. L. Deinstitutionalization of the developmentally disabled. In J. L. Paul, R. Wiegerink, and G. R. Neufeld (Eds.), *Advocacy: A Role for DD Councils*. Chapel Hill, N.C.: DDTAS, 1975.

Stewart, A., Lafave, H. G., Grunberg, F., and Herjanic, M. Problems in phasing out a large public psychiatric hospital. *American Journal of Psychiatry*, 1968, *125(1)*, 120–126.

15

Service Delivery in Rural Areas: Context, Problems, and Issues

Charles Horejsi

Efforts to develop community-based programs in rural areas must grapple with problems and issues somewhat different from those encountered in urban areas. Unfortunately, the special needs and problems of rural areas do not get much attention. Popp (1974) noted that the

> special needs of rural areas seem to have been neglected in the nation's efforts to recognize and cope with the problems of mentally retarded persons. When the federal government arranged in 1964 for "comprehensive" state-wide mental retardation studies throughout the country, only a very few states ever mentioned the specific needs existing in rural areas. Yet rural areas still comprise a large part of the nation (p. 129).

Cochran (1976) has offered convincing arguments concerning the existence of a pro-urban and possibly an anti-rural bias within various federal agencies, including the Department of Health, Education and Welfare. Copp (1970) made similar observations. This bias results from the fact that most of those in decision-making positions are from urban areas, now live in urban areas, have work experience in urban programs, received their professional education in urban universities, and hear and read most about urban problems and programs. They are simply uninformed about rural areas. They are more familiar with what is going on in urban areas and how things work in urban areas. If one wishes to view it from a behavioral point of view, one could conclude they have not been rewarded for paying attention to people from rural areas, or, conversely, they have been rewarded for paying attention to urban areas.

A 1966 Wisconsin project identified a number of special problems relating to the development of community-based programs for mentally retarded persons in rural areas:

A. In a rural area the understanding and awareness of retarded persons' needs and the subsequent impetus to serve them has suffered from the relative lack of exposure to publicity, information, and educational effort.

B. Services for the retarded have not developed in rural areas due to the mechanical problems involved in bringing people together in an area of low population density.

C. In a rural area there is often a lack of facilities, such as day care, sheltered workshops, and special classes, to serve the retarded.

D. Most rural areas lack diagnostic and treatment centers.

E. Rural areas lack an organizational structure for proper identification, treatment, and referral of the retarded and their families.

F. There is an extreme lack of trained professionals, such as psychologists, social workers, public health nurses, and physicians, who can offer service to the retarded or their families.

G. The rural retarded and their families have long been unaware of any alternatives to strict custodial care in the home.

H. People in rural areas often have low expectations for their normal child, as well as the retarded, and are unable to see the value of training and education.

I. There is often a stigma attached to family counseling in a rural area, and the fixed point of referral may be located in a clinic or welfare department. Where little stigma is attached, such as the public health nursing service, this office is understaffed in a rural area.

J. Neighbors in a rural area often have less experience with and understanding of the retarded child than their urban counterparts.

K. Parents of the retarded in a rural area are often poor and cannot afford the cost involved in transportation or the child care necessary to attend parent group meetings or take advantage of counseling and diagnostic services for their retarded child (cited in Popp, 1975, pp. 129-130).

Ten years later, most of these problems still exist in rural areas. If services and opportunities are to be expanded for persons who are developmentally disabled and living in rural areas, planning and program development must be built upon rural resources and characteristics. Moreover, we need to reexamine our tendency to try and "export" urban planning concepts and urban programs into rural areas. Rather, our strategies and tactics must be individualized to local circumstances and the rural condition.

According to Mayeda (1971), several local and state characteristics must be considered in the development of a comprehensive service system for the mentally retarded. These are: 1) land area, 2) population, 3) consumer resources, 4) professional resources, 5) organizational resources, 6) consumer or client characteristics, and 7) transportation. The remainder of this chapter focuses on several of these factors and elaborates on some of the problems and issues of program development and service delivery in rural areas.

WHAT IS A RURAL AREA?

In the United States three-fourths of the people live on about 30% of the land. According to Kahn (1973):

> About half the people of the country live in eight of the fifty states— California, Illinois, Michigan, New Jersey, New York, Ohio, Pennsylvania and Texas. Most of that half, furthermore, live in or just outside the big cities of the eight states. However, the other side of the story is that a large number of Americans live in nonmetropolitan areas.

About 64 million Americans, one-third of our population, live in nonmetropolitan areas. More precisely, they did not live in a Standard Metropolitan Statistical Area, i.e., a metropolitan area surrounding a city with a population of at least 50,000.

Essentially, a rural area is characterized by spareness of population or a low density. In other words, it is a relatively large land area occupied by a relatively small number of people. A few facts and figures on my own state of Montana will serve to clarify this definition.

In physical size, Montana is the fourth largest state; it is approximately 550 miles long and 315 miles wide. The states of Iowa, Indiana, Kentucky, Maryland, and New Jersey could all "fit" in Montana. The 1973 estimated population for the entire state was 721,000. About 50 metropolitan areas in the United States have populations exceeding the population of the whole state of Montana. Only 17 Montana towns have populations over 5,000. Only seven have populations over 10,000. The state's two largest metropolitan areas have populations of about 80,000 each. The third largest city has a population of about 35,000. Nearly every town with a population over 5,000 is at least 100 miles from a community of equal size or larger.

THE RURAL CONDITION

Increasingly, the rural community resembles urban or suburban communities (Warren, 1972). While traditional urban-rural differences are becoming blurred, remnants of a rural culture still exist. Rogers and Burdge (1972), for example, note that rural people (mainly farmers and ranchers) exhibit certain attitudes and values that are different from those of people in urban areas. In areas where rural culture still persists, it must be considered in planning and service delivery.

Rural culture and characteristics have obvious relevance to the design and management of services in accord with the normalization principle. Bronston (1976) states that:

> The essence of that principle requires the use of *culturally normative means and methods . . .* to offer a person *life conditions at least as good as the average citizen . . . and as much as possible enhance or support his/her behavior experiences, status and reputation.* By *culturally normative means,* we speak about using those techniques, tools, media, and methods that are most familiar and valued in our culture (p. 495).

Since the application of the normalization principle is "culture specific," it is interesting to ponder questions such as: 1) What are the "normal" conditions of the average rural citizen? and 2) To what extent should programs in rural areas incorporate the life experiences, values, and expectations of rural people?

Ginsberg (1973) has identified a number of conditions which are "normal" for the typical rural American. Some are the following:

> Rural dwellers often lack access to high quality education, highways, museums, libraries and entertainment . . . In a small town the choice [of entertainment] may be between a few bars and one movie.

> There is simply not much to do with one's free time . . . The rural wealthy may take world cruises or fly to a city for the weekend but the rural dweller of moderate means lacks such choices.

> If one is seriously ill the nearest urban hospital may be used, with all the attendant problems of transportation, isolation from family and friends and the added expense.

> Some small towns have no physicians or dentists. Others must rely on circuit riding healers, who serve each of several small towns one or two days a week . . . Still others must make do with less adequately prepared professionals than they could find in cities.

> Rural communities tend to be one or two industry or company towns (e.g., farming, agribusiness, mining). Frequently, the industries are unattractive to young men and women.

> Many rural areas, perhaps most, lack efficient, low cost public transportation. But the available jobs may be miles away. Thus, ownership of an automobile is often a necessity for a worker in a rural area.

> One has little difficulty in finding overt racial segregation, lack of suffrage, corruption . . . Rural governments are often run by the local power structure much in keeping with the descriptions . . . found in the writings of Floyd Hunter (1969). The Lions Club, Rotary Club, Methodist Church and city council are frequently governed by the local wealthy citizens, no matter who the officially designated presidents, mayors or councilmen are.

> American Indians, Chicanos, and Blacks continue to report being singled out for special punishment by local law enforcement officials who are products of the same power elite that control everything else . . . no case is being

made to support the idea that rural officials are less concerned about human rights than their counterparts in cities. However, cities have a number of other institutions such as civil rights organizations, legal aid agencies and government offices that conduct monitoring activities that, in turn, make officials responsive to the protection of human rights and less inclined to act inappropriately. Rural communities are too small to support such institutions.

. . . the church plays a major role in rural communities, perhaps a greater one than in urban areas. One's religious affiliation is an important consideration for newcomers to small towns.

Impersonal services are uncommon in a setting where everyone knows everyone else or at least everyone else's relatives.

. . . taking social or political positions that differ from those dictated by the conventional wisdom of the rural community may lead to social and professional ostracism.

Those who are too quick to tell others their faults are unpopular in both the metropolis and the village. But the results of such behavior are more rapid, persuasive and dramatic in the (rural community) (pp. 3–7).

What does all this mean? It means that there are both positives and negatives associated with most rural characteristics and norms. It does not mean that those of us interested in expanding services for the developmentally disabled should unquestionably support all rural norms. We must, however, be able to understand and accept those norms and work for change at a pace acceptable to the rural people themselves.

THE FORMAL AND INFORMAL SERVICES OF RURAL AREAS

Recent contributions to social service literature (see, for example, Buxton, 1973; Koch, 1973; Mermelstein and Sundet, 1973; Miller, 1976; Segal, 1973) have identified several features of service delivery that are unique to rural areas. The literature also indicates that strategies and programs developed in urban areas cannot be simply "transplanted" into rural areas or small towns.

While it is true that rural communities have fewer formally organized professional services and agencies, it is a serious error to assume that a particular service is not being provided simply because a formal organization does not exist to provide that service (Ginsberg, 1973). It is important to remember that informal systems of service are common to rural areas. Patterson and Twente (1971) term these informal arrangements "natural service systems" or "natural helpers." More recently, the National Association of Social Workers published a book on natural helping networks (Collins and Pancoast, 1976). These natural service systems include neighbor helping neighbor, loans among friends, service club involvement in helping specific families or specific handicapped individuals, and hiring people who need a job rather than people who have the skills. These informal arrangements tend to develop in the absence of formal services. The rural professional must win access to the natural service system and ensure that his formal and agency-based approach works in accord with the informal arrangements. This means developing and nurturing friendly relationships with local ministers, physicians, teachers, service clubs, agricultural extension agents, and community leaders. It has been observed that service clubs play an especially important role in the informal delivery system at the local level (Ginsberg, 1969). These informal networks lack the sophistication and knowledge base of professionally organized programs, but they do perform a valuable function and are usually "supported" by the influential citizens and community leaders making up the power structure. If a new formal plan for the development of human services poses a threat to these informal service structures, it may encounter considerable resistance. However, Wylie (1973) has observed that this informal helping network may be more of an asset than a liability in developing a new formal service system in rural areas:

> Here is a mighty resource for the social planner, a pool of people accustomed to helping each other, a pool of people already accepted and identified by the community as helping agents, and people who can be easily identified . . . the challenge is to strengthen and expand this natural network by preserving the naturalness rather than imposing professional standards and norms. In other words, . . . what we have there already may be quite good in its own right (p. 26).

Despite some obstacles to change in rural areas, unique potentials are also present. One is the sense of pride and community spirit that exists in many rural areas. These elements are especially strong in relation to self-help activities and "taking care of our own." If new program ideas and plans are generated from within the community and are supported by respected citizens, the rural community is capable of rapid and surprisingly innovative action. On the other hand, plans or programs that are imposed upon small communities by "outsiders" often meet with passive resistance or fail to win support necessary for implementation. Thus, it is essential that parents, "natural helpers," and members of the power structure be involved in any planning process that affects rural communities. Not only is their involvement necessary to win acceptance of new concepts and new programs but many of these same individuals are needed to form the nucleus of volunteers that is so necessary to rural programs. As one might expect, it is no small task for regional or state planners to strike a balance between a community's unique desires and values and the bureaucratic requirements of large-scale social planning and funding constraints.

Those wishing to escape the urban scene should not move to a rural community expecting an uncomplicated life. The dynamics of rural communities are far from simple:

> Rural communities are often as sociologically complex as urban communities. Many of their characteristics may be based upon little remembered but nevertheless influential historical events focused on family conflicts, church schisms, and a variety of other occurrences which may deserve the status of legends (Ginsberg, 1969, p. 30).

Unless someone in the community chooses to inform you of these "historical events," you may live in a community for many years and remain baffled at the local behavior and the patterns of cooperation and noncooperation.

The "history" of interpersonal relations in the small community has an obvious effect on service delivery. Who runs or staffs a program may have much to do with whether or not a particular service is utilized by particular families. Thus, in the selection of staff, their personal background or "image" in the community is of critical importance, sometimes of more importance than their professional competence.

The provision of services on the Indian reservations common to many rural areas presents an even greater challenge. Cultural difference and intertribal conflicts can completely baffle the White, middle class professional or social planner. The usual approaches to service delivery and notions of professional/client relations are contrary to the tradition of noninterference. Good Tracks (1973) explains noninterference as follows:

> In native American society, no interference or meddling of any kind is allowed or tolerated, even when it is to keep the other person from doing something foolish or dangerous. When an Anglo is moved to be his brother's keeper and that brother is an Indian, therefore, everything he says or does seems rude, ill-mannered or hostile.
>
> . . . the Indian child is taught that complete noninterference with all people is the norm, and that he should react with amazement, irritation, mistrust and anxiety to even the slightest indication of manipulation or coercion (pp. 30–31).

The value we place on early intervention, crisis intervention, behavior modification, parent training, and advocacy indicates that most of us have been taught that interference is acceptable, even desirable.

THE RURAL FAMILY

It is difficult, perhaps impossible, to formulate valid generalizations about the rural family. Clearly, rural families are experiencing the same stresses and strains that affect all modern families. Yet there are hints that there are a few differences between urban and rural families. Rogers and Burdge (1972) state:

The family is changing, but rural families have tended to lag behind urban families on many of the trends and changes taking place. For example, rural families are still larger in size than urban families; they have retained more of the traditional family functions, are more father-centered and have fewer divorces (pp. 194–195).

Our approaches to service delivery should recognize such differences and build upon them. Berkley (1976), for example, has observed how the tradition of hospitality can be utilized in gathering research and diagnostic data from rural families:

Refusing hospitality is a gross mistake in a rural setting. I was always served tea or coffee and frequently was invited to stay for meals. Mealtime is usually the only time the entire family is assembled at once. The atmosphere around the table is much more relaxed and decidedly more information can be obtained . . . than in a formal interview setting (p. 3).

Berkley also states that many rural families felt their developmentally disabled child was fairly well accepted by community people:

This observation seemed to come more from persons who had lived in the community . . . for a relatively long period . . . and had established good community relationships . . . There also seems to prevail an air of the "extended family" in rural settings—emotional and psychological support of a family who has a handicapped member comes from friends and neighbors—as contrasted to our "professional extended family" that exists in large urban settings in the form of specialized services and . . . professionals (p. 6).

Because formal human service organizations are few and far between, many rural families have had little or no experience with such organizations. Many do not know how to find or utilize the few services that do exist. Thus, high quality information and referral service and the professional roles of social broker and advocate-ombudsman take on added importance in rural areas.

CONFIDENTIALITY IN SERVICE DELIVERY

Because of the relatively small number of people living in rural communities, the residents know just about everyone around.

Scrutiny of everyone by everyone else is often characteristic of rural communities and what one does in his or her spare time, in the evenings and on weekends, is often a matter of public concern and discussion (Ginsberg, 1973, p. 9).

That lack of privacy and anonymity presents some obvious problems for both the client and the professional.

The client or potential client may worry that everyone will know that he is seeking professional help. So long as the services sought are for rather tangible problems (e.g., physical therapy, medical treatment) there seem to be few conflicts. If, however, the individual needs professional help with personal or family problems, social or emotional ones, he may avoid being seen at agencies or offices providing such assistance. While working in a rural area of Colorado, this author observed that some individuals and families preferred to drive 50 or 60 miles to a "strange town" in order to keep appointments with traveling mental health teams even though the team was in their own community on a regular basis.

The rural professional is often placed in the rather awkward position of serving on committees or attending social and community gatherings with his clients. This can make both client and worker a bit uncomfortable, especially if they have shared highly personal matters.

PROFESSIONAL RESOURCES

Rural communities can rarely support or afford a variety of professionals with specialized knowledge or skills. Thus, as is true for most human service professionals in rural areas, the professional working in rural programs for the developmentally disabled is forced by circumstances to become somewhat of a generalist. Few are able to specialize. Most rural professionals work with clients having a wide variety of problems and needs and most must carry administrative, planning, and community organization responsibilities in addition to direct service duties.

The author has observed a fairly high rate of burn-out among professionals in rural areas, especially those who must do extensive traveling. Burn-out is probably also related to the breadth of their duties and feelings that they have to know a little about everything but are denied the satisfaction of feeling they are really competent in one special area.

Because specialists are not available and because rural professionals have fewer opportunities to function as members of teams, they need to have a broader knowledge base and a greater range of skills than their urban counterparts. Very important skills are those related to the training and utilization of the volunteers and paraprofessionals who must often carry heavy responsibilities in rural programs. Programs in continuing education and staff development are vital to agencies that are staffed by many nonprofessionals and by professionals who must carry a wide range of responsibilities.

It is also important to note that the professional in rural areas must often assume roles quite unlike those he might have in a large metropolitan area. In comparison to urban areas, rural area residents place less value on professional credentials and "expert opinion." Whether or not a professional's suggestions are accepted often depends on his informal behavior and how he relates to "ordinary people" in social situations.

Because many professionals live and work in small, isolated communities, they often suffer from loneliness and a lack of professional stimulation. Supervision and consultation are often unavailable. Professional organizations are generally weak because of the small number of professionals in any one community and the great distances between communities. Agency libraries, if they exist at all, are usually inadequate.

Because so few agencies offer employment opportunities, rural workers are understandably reluctant to engage in actions that might jeopardize their jobs (e.g., advocacy, public criticism of the "system"). A protest resignation or an involuntary loss of one's job because of "boat rocking" often means that the worker must abandon employment in the human service field or leave the state to secure similar employment.

Unusual dress and unorthodox behavior can have an immediate and devastating effect upon a professional's ability to function in the community. Community acceptance is precious and essential to the rural practitioner, and it must be nurtured constantly. Community acceptance comes slowly and is based almost entirely on personal and informal behavior rather than professional credentials, previous experience, or formal education. A newcomer to an area is always treated as an outsider. It may take years before he feels a part of the community.

ECONOMIC ISSUES IN RURAL AREAS

It is commonly assumed that a "unit" of social or human service costs about four times more in a rural area than in an urban area. This unit cost includes both the direct or indirect costs to the client (e.g., fees, time away from work, travel expense) and the agency. The expenses of travel by staff and/or clients are key factors that increase the cost of service.

A lack of coordination among community programs is a common problem within all human service networks, including the developmental disabilities service system. A major cause of this problem is the multiple sources of private, county, state, and federal funding utilized in the provision of services. Each source has guidelines that regulate the use of funds, the type of service that can be provided, and eligibility. Thus, coordinated funding appears to be a prerequisite for a coordinated service delivery system.

The small number of developmentally disabled persons in any one community makes it economically unfeasible for all communities to develop a comprehensive service system. Rather, services must be regionalized.

Ideally, they should be planned and administered at the regional level (Scheerenberger, 1974).

For the rural area, regionalization means the utilization of some type of multicounty organization. Given the fact that most rural communities and counties are rather provincial in their outlook, the creation and maintenance of such an organization can be a frustrating administrative experience but a good education in courthouse politics.

ORGANIZATIONAL RESOURCES IN RURAL AREAS

Purchase of service contracts is commonly used to provide public funding to private organizations. Gilbert and Specht (1974) note that the purchase of service funding mechanism has both advantages and disadvantages:

> The major virtue of these forms of subvention to private and voluntary organizations is that they provide a varied means for starting government programs quickly. They avoid the rigidities of civil service and bureaucracy. Such characteristics are advantageous for public programs for small special groups of clients and for experiments or demonstrations.

> For the voluntary agency, the obvious advantage of these arrangements is access to public coffers as additional sources of income. But they pay a price. To the extent that voluntary agencies are supported by government funds, they forfeit some degree of autonomy. Consequently, these agencies are limited in their ability to function as agents for the expression of new or unpopular ideas, as critics of public services, and as the guardians of pluralistic values. In the extreme, voluntary agencies may simply become an instrument of government policy (p. 150).

In rural areas the flexibility of this mechanism is especially attractive because it permits the shaping and molding of programs to fit local situations, traditions, and values. As previously indicated, programs designed and operated by local people are more likely to be accepted and supported by the community even though they are state funded. The community tends to view them as "out programs." By comparison, state-operated programs have a harder time winning community support.

The purchase of a service mechanism does, however, face some special problems in rural areas. The approach presumes that private human service organizations exist and that they are capable of modifying or expanding their programs to provide purchasable services. Well-established private agencies are rare in rural areas. Those that exist tend to be small and fragile. Many are operated and staffed by volunteers or have a paid staff of one or two people. Because they frequently lack adequate professional resources, these organizations are seldom capable of planning and developing the sophisticated training and behavioral shaping programs needed by the more severely retarded or those with behavioral problems.

Not infrequently, agency board members and key decision makers within these small organizations are unaware of successful programs in other parts of the country. Innovations or program changes are more likely to be based on the experience of a program in a nearby community than on ideas derived from national conferences or from professional literature.

In some cases, a new nonprofit corporation is created for the specific purpose of securing public funds for the provision of badly needed services. Unfortunately, a newly created organization must devote most of its time and energy to maintenance functions. Only after it "gets on its feet" is it capable of devoting full attention to providing service. Thus, a new private service organization in a rural community may have a difficult time adhering to performance standards established by the state funding agency. This places state agencies in an awkward position of funding programs that leave much to be desired in the way of high quality services.

ARCs (Associations for Retarded Citizens) and other self-help or consumer groups in rural areas are usually small and relatively weak. Physical distance between families and the reality that there is a finite limitation on human energy and commitment makes it difficult to muster and maintain a stable advocate organization. In another example from Montana, the ARC has two paid staff members, an Executive Director and a Secretary/ Assistant. That is not much of a staff to cover a large state. Travel budgets are phenomenal.

CONCLUSION

Rural areas are different from urban areas. Programs and services developed in metropolitan areas and designed to serve persons living in urban areas simply cannot be replicated or "transplanted" in rural areas or in a small community. Rural-urban differences must be recognized. Planning and service delivery in rural areas must be built upon the rural culture and characteristics.

REFERENCES

Berkley, A. The rural family as service consumer. Paper presented at the 100th Annual Meeting of the American Association on Mental Deficiency, May 30–June 4, 1976, Chicago, Illinois.

Bronston, W. Concepts and theory of normalization. In R. Koch and J. Dobson (Eds.), *The Mentally Retarded Child and His Family*. Rev. ed. New York: Brunner/Mazel, Inc., 1976.

Buxton, E. Delivering social services in rural areas. *Public Welfare*, 1973, *31*, 15–20.

Cochran, C. Rural America: A time for decision. Paper presented at the First National

Institute on Social Work in Rural Areas: Preparation and Practice. University of Tennessee, School of Social Work, July 13–16, 1976, Knoxville, Tennessee.

Collins, A., and Pancoast, D. *Natural Helping Networks*. New York: National Association of Social Workers, 1976.

Copp, J. The meanings of rural—a third of our nation. *Contours of Change: The Yearbook of Agriculture*. Washington, D.C.: U.S. Department of Agriculture, 1970.

Gilbert, N., and Specht, H. *Dimensions of Social Welfare Policy*. Englewood Cliffs, N.J.: Prentice-Hall, Inc., 1974.

Ginsberg, L. Education for social work in rural settings. *Social Work Education Reporter*, 1969, *17*.

Ginsberg, L. An Overview of Social Work Education for Rural Areas. In L. Ginsberg, (Ed.) *Social Work in Rural Communities: A Book of Readings*. New York: Council on Social Work Education, 1976.

Ginsberg, L. Planning the delivery of services in rural areas. In W. Koch (Ed.), *Planning and Delivery of Services in Rural America: A Symposium*. University of Wisconsin-Extension: The Center for Continuing Education and Community Action for Social Services, May, 1973.

Good Tracks, J. Native American noninterference. *Social Work*, 1973, *18*, 30–34.

Hunter, F. *Community Power Structure*. Chapel Hill, N.C.: University of North Carolina Press, 1969.

Kahn, E. J. Who, what, where, how much, how many, Part I. *The New Yorker*, 1973, *15*, 137–138.

Koch, W. (ed.). *Planning and Delivery of Social Services in Rural America: A Symposium*. University of Wisconsin-Extension: The Center for Continuing Education and Community Action for Social Services, May, 1973.

Mayeda, T. A. Delivery of services to mentally retarded children and adults in five states. Washington, D.C.: President's Committee on Mental Retardation, January, 1971.

Mermelstein, J., and Sundet, P. Community control and determination of professional role in rural mental health. *Journal of Operational Psychiatry*, Fall-Winter, 1973.

Miller, K. Rural social work in Canada. Paper presented at the First National Institute on Social Work in Rural Areas: Preparation and Practice, July 13–16, 1976, University of Tennessee, School of Social Work, Knoxville, Tennessee.

Patterson, S., and Twente, E. Older natural helpers: Their characteristics and patterns of helping. *Public Welfare*, 1971, *29*, 400–401.

Popp, D. Service delivery in rural areas. In C. Cherington and G. Dybwad (Eds.), *New Neighbors: The Retarded Citizen in Quest of a Home*. Washington, D.C.: U.S. Government Printing Office, 1975.

Rogers, E., and Burdge, R. *Social Change in Rural Societies*. 2nd Ed. Englewood Cliffs, N.J.: Prentice-Hall, Inc., 1972.

Scheerenberger, R. C. A model for deinstitutionalization. *Mental Retardation*, 1974, *12*, 3–7.

Segal, J. (Ed.). *The Mental Health of Rural America*. Washington, D.C.: U.S. Department of HEW, 1973. (DHEW Publication No. HSM 73-9035.)

Warren, R. *The Community in America*. 2nd Ed. Chicago: Rand McNally Co, 1972.

Wylie, M. Social planning in nonmetropolitan America. In W. Koch, (Ed.) *Planning and Delivery of Social Services in Rural America: A Symposium*. University of Wisconsin-Extension: The Center for Continuing Education and Community Action for Social Services, May, 1973.

16

Role of the Consumer in Planning and Delivering Services

Frank Warren

The role of the consumer in planning and delivering services should be obvious to DD Council members. A consumer's needs, as seen by him, should be addressed from the very outset; his wants, and they vary from consumer to consumer, should be taken into serious consideration before any planning begins; and he should not only be consulted, surveyed, studied, and evaluated, but he should be an active participant in the planning process, wielding decision-making power equal to that of professional planners and providers. In short, the consumer should be a participant in every aspect of the planning and delivery of services designed to benefit him or to solve or alleviate the problems that he faces.

This chapter describes some roles for consumers in planning and delivering services and identifies issues related to those roles.

THE CONSUMER

The consumer—the retarded, cerebral palsied, epileptic, or autistic child or adult—is the focus for people in the business of providing assistance for developmentally disabled individuals. When a service is provided for a developmentally disabled child or adult who is in the care of another person, family, or guardian, it becomes a service for those people as well as for the disabled child or adult.

In the majority of cases, parents, families, or guardians are the best advocates for disabled people. As advocates, they speak for them, act in their behalf, and in their best interest. Services for disabled people that meet their real needs also meet the needs of their parents, families, and guardians.

A NEED FOR COOPERATION

In order to facilitate a creative and integral involvement of consumers in the planning and delivery of services, a spirit of mutual trust and cooperation must be nurtured between the consumer and the professional. The consumer cannot know everything the professional has learned after years of study. It is equally true that the professional cannot know everything the consumer has learned after years of being, or living with, a developmentally disabled person, often being put down, turned down, and cooled out by insensitive professionals who do not know what to do, and who will not or cannot admit it, and by the bureaucratized service system.

There must be communication before any kind of constructive cooperation can occur between the professional who is being paid to help and the parent who has a child with special needs. If the professional considers the consumer incompetent, how can he expect to gain the respect and confidence of that consumer? How can they work together? If the parent sees the professional as arrogant and unwilling to listen, how can they cooperate for the good of the child?

In most cases the professionals are organized, have the mandate to provide services, and are supposed to have the ability and the access to technical knowledge. The consumers, on the other hand, are disorganized, are spread out, and are spending most of their time being lawyers, sharecroppers, businessmen, television repairmen, newspaper reporters, filling station operators, secretaries, farmers, or whatever to support their families. It seems only reasonable for the professionals to take the initiative. It is their full-time job to plan and deliver services, and they must take it upon themselves to break down the unnecessary barriers between them and the people they are supposed to serve.

To do this, professionals must look upon the consumer as a valuable person who is doing the best he can within the circumstances of his life. Professionals must give consumers the dignity and respect they deserve as human beings. Make no mistake about it, they deserve it. Professionals must recognize the fact that most parents love their children, want to be near them, want to be good parents to them, and want their problems and handicaps dealt with in sensible, appropriate ways so that they can develop as individuals able to live lives that are as satisfying as possible.

Planners and service deliverers must include the consumer from the beginning—consult him, listen to him, draw upon his knowledge and ability, find out what his real needs and desires are, and use his strength and support to accomplish the goals that they together, consumers and professionals, have established. This is the strongest position to work from. Where this has been done, the results have been invariably good.

Of course this does not mean that consumers should stand idly by until a professional person decides to let them in on what's happening. It is quite appropriate for them to initiate the action, to pound on the door if they have to, in order to participate where they rightfully belong.

While some professionals carefully guard their territory from the intrusion of consumers, this is not always the case. Many professionals involved in planning and delivering services actively seek consumer participation when they are in a position to do so. Many others would be amenable to consumer involvement if the structure of the programs in which they are involved permitted it, or if their particular discipline taught that it was appropriate. Many, in fact, enter a discipline holding a liberal view toward consumer involvement, but emerge from their professional education with that liberal view washed away through long exposure to a system that does not value consumers as participants in planning and delivering services.

Consumers, seeking to have an impact on the systems that are supposed to be serving them, do well to approach professionals as if they were potential friends and allies. Will Rogers said, "Everybody is ignorant—about different things." It may be that the problem is simple ignorance on the part of professionals regarding the value of consumer participation and involvement. When this is the case, it is up to the consumers to educate the professionals. If this is done with tact and persistence from a position of strength, many battles may be avoided and much cooperation gained.

CONSUMER COMMUNICATION, ORGANIZATION, AND ALLIANCES

A common degrading comment made by professionals and people involved in delivering services is that parents do not care; furthermore, they will not participate, you cannot get them involved, they will not come to meetings and conferences, and they are only interested in their own children and nobody else.

To the degree that this is true, it is because parents of developmentally disabled children tend to be isolated, cut off from regular association with others who have the same kinds of problems, and trained by their association with traditional professionals to believe that they are inept and cannot do anything to solve their problems. Many are unaware of the strong effect they can have on professionals and on the services they deliver.

In order for consumers to have some kind of impact on the people who make decisions affecting them and their children, communication and organization must be considered. Communication implies a two-way exchange of facts and ideas. Organization implies a method of continuing the communication. To have any kind of continuing communication among consumers, between consumers and planners, and between consumers and service providers, there must be some form of organization.

Perhaps this sounds too obvious to state, but the fact is that many consumers, overwhelmed by their own problems, are unaware that there are many others who face the same circumstances. They never realize that many problems can be solved and much suffering alleviated through joint action, by letter and phone, through making concerted demands for improved services.

As part of an oppressed minority, the consumer has a powerful platform from which to launch an effort to improve his life circumstances. Many consumers are discriminated against, often having to pay a large price for things, such as education, that other people get free. Both laws and public attitudes exclude the disabled consumer from many things that make life worthwhile. Systems set up at public expense to serve people in a multitude of ways regularly leave disabled persons out. Often the consumer is ignored, circumvented, patronized, taken advantage of, used, pitied, and, in some cases, his rights as a human being and as a citizen are arbitrarily taken from him.

Consumers must join together and direct all of their energies toward changing the laws, attitudes, systems, and individuals that are putting them down and dealing them out. Consumers must organize. To have any kind of impetus and stability, organization must be based on a common need and aimed toward solving common problems. Consumer organizations can take a great variety of forms; a small parent group may come together to solve relatively simple problems in a classroom; wide-flung alliances of existing consumer organizations may be established to change public attitudes, influence and create legislation, alter systems of service delivery to meet the real needs of disabled people, and make an impact on state and federal government.

The first step toward organizing consumers is to realize that there are a number of people, usually isolated from each other and struggling with their problems alone, who have common needs that could be met and common problems that could be solved if they joined resources and acted in unison.

Here are a few guidelines for consumers attempting to develop an effective organization:

Meet regularly.

Encourage those with the greatest commitment and the keenest understanding of the problem to exercise their leadership ability.

Establish a means of regular communication between members. A well-written newsletter can instill enthusiasm, impart valuable information, enlighten the membership, encourage action and provide a constant link with members who may not be able to attend all meetings. Best of all, it is cheap.

Don't bite off more than you can chew. A problem solved well gives credibility to your organization and a sense of accomplishment to members.

On the other hand, don't whittle your goals down to the point that they are worthless. Work toward an ideal, and measure your accomplishments against it.

Don't give up in despair when members of your group fall short of the commitment you think they ought to have. Remember that every member has a different level of commitment to the cause, depending on the circumstances of his life. Rejoice in the participation that you get, and move on.

Don't turn your organization into a vehicle for personal gratification or ego satisfaction. Give credit where credit is due, and dole out praise and encouragement in large quantities—whether it is deserved or not.

Once you have found your consumer element, identified a common problem, and begun to meet, then it is time to make an assessment of what your group wants to accomplish. Start with an ideal. Don't be awed by the task ahead of you. Take it on a piece at a time. Share responsibilities.

Examine existing approaches. It is likely that most of the things your group needs are already being provided to others through systems that are already in operation, but from which your people are excluded. If such is the case, and if these systems are funded by tax money, there is no good reason why they cannot be altered to serve your people as well.

Think long and hard before you decide to work toward the establishment of a separate system to meet the needs of your consumer element, while another, parallel system is serving others but excluding you. Sometimes this has to be done if it is clear that your people would be served inadequately and their special needs lost in the larger system. However, the goal should be to get the needs of your element met in appropriate fashion by the agencies and systems already set up to serve the people.

It is of utmost importance to gather carefully all the facts and information that you can before setting a course of action. Study the alternatives and work toward the solution of your problems in the most appropriate manner.

Use your organization and your systems of communication to let all of your people know what the possibilities are.

Be sure that the goals you set are ones that will meet the real needs of your consumer group.

Then go to work!

More and more it is becoming apparent that consumer organizations must form alliances to gain services and education for developmentally disabled children and adults, services and education that they all commonly need, but that some groups would be hard pressed to get on their own.

It is a disservice to all developmentally disabled people for consumer groups to work alone and cause a separate system to be set up for each group when they could work together, bound by the realization of their common needs. Joint action can result in the establishment of systems that address themselves to the real needs of disabled people rather than to categories of disability.

When categorical service systems are set up, they arbitrarily exclude people on the basis of a label, and not because those people cannot benefit from the service. This is wasteful and it is harmful to the excluded people. An alliance of consumer groups for developmentally disabled people can bring strong leadership together, provide situations in which they can discover areas of common interest, and plan unified action that can benefit all of those concerned.

This is not to say that separate organizations, societies, and associations are not needed. They are essential. They need to be strong and active. Each element of disabled people has special needs that are understood better by them than by anyone else. When they come together in an alliance, however, they can learn more about each other and realize that their areas of common need are vast and the possibilities for unified action are many. Alliances of consumer groups are the wave of the future. They are already being formed. Where they emerge in ways that do not threaten the special needs of individual groups, their impact is substantial and invariably beneficial.

MONITORING AND EVALUATION BY CONSUMERS

One of the best ways for consumers to be sure that services and programs set up to serve them are actually doing the job is through constant monitoring and regular evaluation of these systems and programs. Consumer organizations can monitor classrooms, day care centers, training programs, school boards, town councils, county commissioners, commissions and committees of local and state governments—any service for developmentally disabled persons and any public body with authority to affect the lives of disabled persons.

Consumers, who know what they ought to be receiving from particular programs, are in a good position to make these kinds of judgments. Common sense tells us, and research has borne it out, that people do what they are employed to do with a keener sense of responsibility when they know they are being observed. If the observation is by someone who can intervene in case of laxity or transgression, the sense of responsibility is apt to be heightened considerably.

If consumers are not in a position to correct problems discovered through monitoring and evaluation, they can see to it that an accurate statement of the difficulty is presented to people who can. If the problem is not solved satisfactorily, they can proceed up the line of authority, presenting the problem accurately and firmly at each level, until something is done about it. If all else fails, they can take it to the people through the news media.

Anyone attempting to monitor or evaluate a program must have a clear understanding of how the program is supposed to affect the individuals served by it, what its goals are, and how it goes about meeting them. Standards can be developed from these goals and the program judged on the basis of how well or how poorly it meets these standards. It is elementary that the goals of a program serving disabled people must be those that benefit them directly, meet their needs, and improve the quality of their lives.

Monitoring and evaluation require time, energy, and commitment from consumers. This does not mean that consumer organizations should shy away from doing it. A system of monitoring and evaluation should be an integral part of every program developed to serve disabled people. Consumers involved in planning services can insist that this be done.

Unfortunately, many programs already exist that have no monitoring and evaluation component, and many of these actively resist its installment. It is clearly the responsibility of consumer organizations to overcome this resistance through progressively insistent activity, using strategies adapted to the particular situation, so that program and service delivery systems become clearly accountable to the people they serve, and so that the programs and services are appropriate and beneficial to the consumer.

CONSUMER AND ADVISORY BOARDS

Often it falls to the consumers to take the initiative and use the strength of their combined efforts to turn systems around and make the right things happen. Clear ideas, well-thought-out plans, and plain and sensible proposals designed to fit the real needs of disabled citizens are the best tools to use in altering established systems that are ineffective, if not harmful. When these plans are presented with determination by large numbers of organized consumers, they cannot be ignored.

In recent years, largely as a result of persistent consumer action, the federal government and many state and local governments have begun to recognize the value of consumer participation in the planning and delivery of services. The idea of professionals holding complete control of service delivery systems is slow to die, but much new legislation requires that nonprofessional people serve on boards that plan and direct service delivery.

When this is the case, one of two things can happen. The consumer board member can accept a secondary, passive role in which he becomes a "yes man" to the professionals. When this occurs he has not only negated any value he might have had as a board member, but he has also provided the professionals with license to do whatever they wish with token consumer consent; or, the consumer can take an active role as board member. There are a number of ways in which actively involved consumers can contribute to and influence boards on which they may serve:

Be informed; attend board meetings prepared to offer ideas and suggestions.

Gain a full understanding of the board's purpose, activity, and power.

Insist that clear and complete explanations be given for all of the board's actions.

Insist that money be spent and priorities set in ways that are fair to every consumer element to be served, and that a full accounting be made.

Ensure that committee appointments include fair consumer representation.

See that a minority report is issued if action is taken with which consumer members strongly disagree.

Join with other consumers and take issues to the public through the news media if other channels fail to prevent actions that are felt to be unfair.

An active, informed consumer can give life to a sluggish board and make things happen for the good of the consumers that the board was established to serve. The consumer need not be a parent, guardian, or someone advocating for disabled persons. He may be a disabled person whose disability does not prevent him from being an advocate and who knows, firsthand, about the needs of disabled people.

A consumer serving on a board that is planning services must be cautious not to become so involved with professional people that he adopts the professional attitudes and reactions that have shut consumers out of the planning process and service delivery systems for years. It can happen without his even being aware of it. The result is that the real consumers are shut out once again. They are no longer consulted, since the professional consumer speaks for them. Their real wants and needs go largely unheard. The delivery systems can once again drift into patterns of delivering services that are less and less appropriate to the situations they were designed to alleviate.

A consumer serving on a board that is planning services can avoid the "professional consumer" pitfall by observing a few simple "dos" and "don'ts":

Don't assume that because you are a consumer you automatically know everything every other consumer knows. Be confident that your own viewpoint and your own experiences are valuable. Express that viewpoint and share those experiences, but understand that they may not be universal.

Don't speak for all members of your consumer element until you have a real grasp of what their needs and wants are. Make every effort to know their needs.

Do consider that you are a representative of the consumer group of which you are a part. As a representative, you have a duty to see that consumers are contacted, talked with, involved, polled, and listened to, and that their needs are met by the services you help provide.

Do insist that every element of any program you help design has consumer input and involvement, and that every element is accountable to the people it serves.

If these points are observed, the plans and services that emerge from the work of the board will be much more likely to respond to the real needs of the consumer.

SUMMARY

Consumers, whether they are disabled or advocates for the disabled, have the right and the obligation to play a leading role in the planning and delivery of services that affect their lives. They have a right to know that their share of the tax dollars is spent in ways that are beneficial to them. Consumers have the same obligation as other citizens to see that this occurs.

Professionals must recognize the value of the consumer as a participant in planning and delivering services. They must encourage his participation and respect his ability so that, together, they can accomplish things in which they are commonly interested.

Consumers themselves must unite their efforts. When they are separated, in competition with each other, ignorant of their potential power, they can be overlooked, mistreated, preyed upon, and used by people who have things in mind other than the well-being of the disabled person. When consumers come together with determination to solve their problems, they can become a potent and influential force that cannot be ignored.

The DD Council provides an excellent forum for consumer initiative. Here, consumers can be key members of groups responsible for planning, developing, and improving the quality of services for developmentally disabled people. The Council can also provide support for consumers at the local level in securing their rightful places in service delivery activities. Finally, the Council can be a source of information to consumers and a resource for incorporating local consumer data and perspective at the state level.

17

Consumer Involvement
in Human Services

Ronald Wiegerink, Vince Parrish, and Iris Buhl

The developmental disabilities acts of 1970 and 1975 clearly recognized the important role of the consumer. By requiring that at least one-third of the membership of Developmental Disabilities Councils be consumers, it provided the Council with a very important resource. In addition, of course, it provided the consumer with opportunities to take an active role in planning for the development of comprehensive services for developmentally disabled citizens. The DD amendments of 1978 have increased the role of consumer involvement by requiring that at least one-half of the membership be consumers. In these three acts the roles of consumers in advice-giving, planning, and advocating have been recognized as important functions.

Neglected are the function of service giving and service monitoring, in which consumers can also play an important, if not indispensable, part. In a few places across the country, these functions have been recognized and field tested with very promising results. It is hoped that these results will be replicated and improved upon elsewhere.

There are several substantial reasons for involving consumers and consumer representatives, namely, parents, in service delivery systems for the developmentally disabled, including: 1) parents know their own children best and this knowledge can be used to good advantage by others working with the children; 2) often parents spend more time with their children than do others, and this time can be used to work with their children in a manner consistent with the center's goals; 3) parents can be of significant help to one another in that they share similar problems and can identify with and support one another; 4) parents can provide the program staff with ongoing evaluative feedback, which can assist the program in being accountable and in making programmatic decisions; 5) parents can provide child behavioral data that can be used to monitor intervention effectiveness; 6) parents supply a source of manpower not readily available from other sources because of the lack of finances and training.

Each of these points is worth elaborating upon and most of them have been explored by other authors (Ora and Reisinger, 1971). Clearly, there are not sufficient services for handicapped children. Even though services have increased rapidly since the Bureau of Education for the Handicapped and the developmental disabilities acts came into being, at the rate services are expanding it will be decades before all of the developmentally disabled are provided with comprehensive services. There are many reasons for this state of affairs; two principal reasons are a lack of financial resources to provide programs for developmentally disabled children and a lack of trained personnel. To accelerate the provision of services, programs are needed that provide high quality services for developmentally disabled children at low costs and do not rely completely on professionally trained practitioners for all or even most of the intervention services. For example, programs currently being funded by the Handicapped Children's Early Education Program are averaging over $3,000 per child served and a ratio of fewer than six children served for the equivalent of each full-time professionally trained staff member. While these costs, in terms of money and manpower, are not too great for a society to spend to assist handicapped children, at present our society is not willing to make these kinds of resources available to serve all developmentally disabled children. Therefore, professionally trained persons who have the responsibility for providing services for all developmentally disabled children must develop and implement service systems that are likely to provide high quality services with substantially lower financial and human resources.

Parents are one source of such human resources. They are readily available. They are already engaged in preparing and teaching their children and are eager to learn more effective ways to rear their children and prepare them to live in society.

OVERVIEW

A project that recognized the value of this human resource early in its inception is the Regional Intervention Program (RIP) of Nashville, Tennessee. This program was one of the first group of projects funded by the Bureau for the Education of the Handicapped under the Handicapped Children's Early Education Program in 1969.

The description of RIP is here presented both as information and encouragement to those interested in developing programs utilizing effective, low-cost consumer participation. While admittedly detailed, the description allows the Council member to examine the steps through which the service delivery system was developed and clearly demonstrates the integral part that can be played by consumers in maintaining such a system. Perhaps it will suggest some viable answers to specific questions of how a similar program might be implemented.

The Regional Intervention Program was described by its first director as "a social experiment in which an agency of people, the Tennessee Department of Mental Health, in cooperation with Peabody College and the Nashville Junior League, provides the citizens of the state with a permanent organizational structure, with support for that structure, and with continuity of information within that structure, but the citizens themselves implement the organization to provide services to their children to their own satisfaction" (Ora, 1972a).

The program serves developmentally disabled and behaviorally disordered preschool children from birth to 5 years of age from a 26-county mental health catchment area. Children and their families are referred to RIP by mental health centers, pediatricians, general practitioners, public health nurses, welfare workers, parents, and other agents and agencies when the family is no longer able to cope with the behavior and learning problems of the child. The time between contact with the project and the beginning of service to the family ranges in most cases from 20 minutes to 48 hours. Thus, RIP is a flexible service system always ready to admit additional families on a no-reject basis. If the family feels it can profit from the services of the program it is always admitted.

The decision to become this flexible has meant that RIP had to design a system for delivering services that is capable of readily providing for new families at any time. Although RIP was originally designed to provide service through the vehicle of professionals, the utilization of parents in the service delivery system soon became a matter of necessity and desirability. A consumer-implemented service system gradually evolved wherein consumers provide all direct service and monitoring of the program, with the support provided by five professionally trained special educators. Designed and implemented as such, it is possible for the project staff (made up of parents and professionals) to provide comprehensive services for approximately 50 additional families during each year of operation. Comprehensive services include transportation, intake, parent training, individual tutoring, preschool classrooms, day care for siblings, medical and behavioral consultation, home visits, liaison with the social service agencies, placement, and follow-along. Through these services, RIP's one objective is to prepare the family and the child for the child's maintenance and developmental progress outside of institutional care. This goal is realized if the child continues to make progress after being placed in a regular day care program or public school classroom.

In order to meet this objective and deliver services, RIP is organizationally divided into functional modules, which achieve management objectives (Figure 1). Each module is supervised by a resource person who has had professional training, but all the services are provided by parents who have

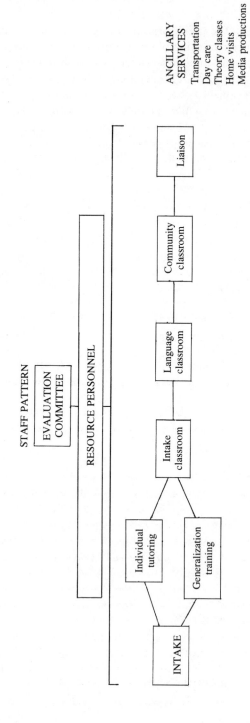

Figure 1. Regional intervention program.

been served by RIP. The entire project is monitored and evaluated by an Evaluation Committee consisting of three parents and three consultants who are selected by the parents through procedures established by the committee or parents. This committee meets regularly and has the responsibility for approving and generating project policies and evaluating ongoing activities. All project personnel meet with the committee at least monthly to report on module activities and individual family progress.

The committee in turn transmits a monthly report, consisting of the minutes of its meeting and its comments on the meeting, to the Coordinator, Preschool Programs Branch, Division of Children and Youth Services, Department of Mental Health. The Coordinator's Office has already perceived that such a system permits extremely close and politically astute monitoring with minimum administrative overhead.

The second level of the program is the professional resource staff, which provides a middle-management function within the project. Each staff member in this level has specified areas of responsibility, which are outlined by management objectives following the format of Reddin's *Effective Management by Objectives* (1971). For example, the principle of RIP is responsible for the overall administrative operations of the program. The professional staff personnel do not provide conventional special education services themselves. They work individually with parents and children only for the purposes of modeling and training, but most direct services are provided by trained parents with whom these resource personnel continuously consult, train, monitor, evaluate, and direct. Essentially, the professional staff members are consultants, providing expertise and personal support for planning and teaching, to parents who are responsible for the implementation of the program.

The third level of the program is delivery of services, which is totally parent implemented. At this level are parents who have received training to work with their own children and have demonstrated particular expertise in at least two domains: technical and interpersonal competence. Their technical competence is, of course, constantly growing and may be in one or more areas of project services, such as intake interviews, child assessment, classroom teaching, individual tutoring, home visits, and child management. In every case, however, these consumers have demonstrated that they can operate within a management-by-objectives framework and can reliably utilize the data collection procedures of RIP. At the center of all RIP services is the importance of objectives and data-based evaluation.

Individual factors, such as personality style, interpersonal skills, and interests, are also considered in determining what responsibilities and functions the parent is to have. These decisions are made by the parents who have provided the new grant with services along with the resource personnel.

Demands for a variety of regional treatment services, constantly shifting referral patterns, and multiple funding sources over the past 5 years have largely determined the numbers and kinds of clients served by the RIP program. The following description of the current program in terms of its clients and referral base will, it is hoped, be a useful reference to those interested in the evolution of the Regional Intervention Program.

Between June, 1969, and March 21, 1974, RIP served a total of 254 families. At present, approximately 40 families are actively enrolled in the program with an approximate average attendance rate of 65%. Thus, about 26 families daily participate in the program. These families have an average of 1.6 preschool children who attend RIP, bringing the program's daily attendance to approximately 26 adults and 40 children.

The average RIP child is 41 months old upon referral and generally will remain in the program for 8.1 months.

During these 5 years, most of the referrals (76% to 80%) were males and approximately one-half of RIP's current referrals could be classified as seriously developmentally delayed. That is, significant delay existed in the language, motoric, and cognitive areas. The remainder of the children were nondevelopmentally delayed, severely behaviorally disordered children who typically were referred to as "brats," oppositional or hyperactive children.

Currently, 24% of RIP's families are Black, having been typically referred by local welfare department social workers, public health department nurses, child development clinics, and, occasionally, a private pediatrician.

In the first 2 years of operations RIP relied very heavily on local pediatricians from the metropolitan Nashville area for referrals (in 1970-71, 76% of all of RIP's referrals originated from pediatricians). However, from 1975 through 1978 the pediatric referral rate has stabilized between 25% and 29% as more mental health centers, social service organizations, and hospital-affiliated diagnostic clincis began to refer to the program. Thus, the program is now fairly representative of the general population of the middle Tennessee area, with 38% of its families in an income range below $7,000, 51% between $7,000 and $13,000, and 11% above $13,000 annual income. Furthermore, as awareness of the program has grown, more families from rural middle Tennessee are daily attending RIP. At present, nearly 25% of the program's families travel more than 50 miles per day (round trip) for services, and some of these commute over 100 miles per day.

PARENT TRAINING—RECAPITULATION

In RIP, parent training and project services are the same; the entire project is designed to help parents help themselves and other parents. Parents are first taught to collect data systematically, using baseline and multiple baseline recording procedures, for the purpose of tutoring their child and evaluating the child's progress in the preschool classrooms. Next, parents are taught the essential skills of behavior modification, reinforcement, timing, shaping, fading, stimulus selection, and programming. As they demonstrate their behavior competencies they begin to receive instruction in the general theories of behaviorism as presented by Skinner (1953) and Bijou and Baer (1961). They then learn more about child development, primarily focusing on language development, but also upon social and motor development.

Once their child is making steady progress and parents have demonstrated competency in some of the basic skills, they begin to offer volunteer services, which can be the beginning of a new career for some. If the parent has demonstrated mastery in individual tutoring or generalization training, he can begin as an assistant in these modules. If parents showed interests in one of the preschool classrooms, they could begin an assistantship there. In some cases, the parents teach others to collect basic behavioral data, but if they show programming and decision-making competencies they can take on more and more responsibilities in one of the service modules.

In most cases parents finish their 6 months of volunteer service and leave the service-giving aspects of the program. Some, however, stay on with the, program as assistants, or in some cases where particular skills and interests are shown, as paid employees responsible for a service module (e.g., Intake Preschool). In some few cases, having demonstrated a good grasp of all functions of RIP, they would take on greater responsibilities, such as directing the Intake or Liaison modules or being responsible for parent coordination and assignment. In a few select cases, some of these parents would become members of the Evaluation Committee, or would, with the additional professional training, become full-time resource personnel. Within the program all parents learn important and valuable competencies which they have an opportunity to use continuously in positions of their own choice.

CONCLUSION

Developmental Disabilities Councils could increase consumer involvement in the planning, development, delivery and monitoring of services if they were to do any of the following:

1. Hold public hearings and have consumers and parents express needs
2. Establish hotlines for consumers to give and gain information
3. Hold systematically sampled interviews with consumers
4. Require that projects funded with DD funds involve consumers in their planning process
5. Require that projects funded by DD funds have consumers on their advisory boards

6. Require that projects funded by DD funds have ongoing monitoring by consumer committees

REFERENCES

Bijou, S. W., and Baer, D. M. *Child Development I: A Systematic and Empirical Theory*. New York: Appleton-Century-Crofts, 1961.

Ora, J.P. Final report for the regional intervention project for preschoolers and parents, December 31, 1972a. Grant No. OEG-0-9-520320-4535 (618).

Ora, J.P. The involvement and training of parent and citizen-workers in early education for the handicapped and their implication: A working paper for the Council on Exceptional Children, Invisible College on Early Childhood. January 20–21, 1972b, San Antonio, Texas.

Ora, J. P., and Reisinger, J. Preschool intervention: Behavioral service delivery system. Paper presented at the American Psychological Association, September, 1971, Washington, D.C.

Reddin, W. J. *Effective Management by Objectives*. New York: McGraw-Hill Book Co., 1971.

Regional Intervention Program Slide Show. Composed, edited and reviewed by the Regional Intervention Staff from 1970–1974.

Skinner, B. F. *Science and Human Behavior*. New York: Macmillan Publishing Co., 1953.

18

Future of Service Delivery Systems for Handicapped Individuals

Donald J. Stedman and Ronald Wiegerink

For nearly 200 years the United States has been attempting to devise an effective program of services for handicapped individuals in the communities. However, only since 1950 have significant strides in the direction of comprehensive services been taken. Only during the last decade have notable achievements been reached.

Part of the progress has been made because national attention has been drawn to the nearly 25 million persons in our society who have special needs due to some handicapping condition. Much of the gain has been a result of expanded research in the area of human development and rehabilitation. A large amount of the success is due to comprehensive approaches to health, social, and educational problems and issues taken from the national level. Major generic programs, such as social security, the poverty program, economic development, comprehensive health and insurance, and programs designed to improve the quality of life, all help identify and reduce the incidence and impact of handicaps on the person and society.

Special federal and state legislation, and consequent service program development, from the time of the Kennedy administration to the present day—notably the comprehensive mental health-mental retardation laws, the veterans administration laws, the economic opportunity act, the rehabilitation act, the civil rights act, the maternal and child health laws, the facilities construction laws, and the developmental disabilities act—have created a fabric of activity that sets the stage for effective action.

The climate for providing services to meet the needs of the developmentally disabled is now more promising than ever before. Most of the needed legislation, legal decision, and monies are now available and ready to be used and accessed. The primary services needed by the developmentally disabled are known; they need to be put in place. There is the rub. Present funding and service configurations are not designed to readily facilitate the development of comprehensive services at the local level where they are provided. Instead, federal and state mandates and categorical funding often serve the opposite purpose; they thwart comprehensive coordinated services. Just as laws and resources have been made available to provide for the disabled, so too should the necessary service configurations. In order to provide these service configurations, some current issues must be addressed.

THE INTEGRATION OF HUMAN SERVICE SYSTEMS

There has been an ever-expanding rhetoric on the integration of human service systems over the last few years. General statements of problems and goals constitute the bulk of the statements coming from all levels, both public and private. Essentially, the discussions and presentations on the "integration of services" and the need for an improved method of integration and coordination amount to a body of general belief or prevailing philosophy that is commonly held by professionals and the special interest groups, which comprise the constituencies of this effort, especially in the area of handicapped individuals. In a report by Gage (1976) it is stated that the Department of Health, Education and Welfare regards the impact of HEW services as less than the sum of its program parts. This is said to be due to:

a. Service programs are not correlated with a common set of national goals and service objectives.
b. They are not responsive to the multiple needs of the clients that they serve.
c. They are not orchestrated through centralized, comprehensive planning processes at state and local levels.
d. They tend to be narrowly prescribed and rigidly regulated.
e. They not only fail to complement one another, but they typically do not mesh with other federal programs inside or outside of HEW.

In addition, the problem of integrating service programs includes a variety of subfactors. The political value of remaining unique helps maintain a competitiveness between agencies and specialized service programs that works against the integration of human service programs at all levels. The difficulty of developing a common or shared information data base slows down the movement toward attempts to develop better integrated service systems.

The development and implementation of services along strictly disciplinary lines tends to hold up cross-agency or interagency programming. There is also a continued resistance to cross-disciplinary or transdisciplinary training and manpower development. Interdisciplinary service and training programs are badly needed.

At present there is a slow but steady trend toward integrated human services agencies at the local (county) level, which help blend health, mental health, rehabilitation, social services, and other programs rather than maintain the current, separate generic agencies. At the top (the federal level), there is an attempt to blend together health, education, and welfare or social services programs within the Department of Health, Education and Welfare. This situation might well be inverted to the point where a separate, cabinet-level, federal agency would be established for health, for education, and for social services that would provide coordinated planning and the development of criteria, policy, regulations, and monitoring activities for an increasingly integrated system of state and local agencies. In other words, the current situation, in which the local agencies are separate and poorly coordinated and the national agencies are attempting to come into a more blended configuration, should be inverted to separate federal agencies into special cabinet-level programs while the local programs are becoming more blended or integrated. This inversion would allow for a shift away from direct service delivery by federal and state agencies toward a program development, resource development, technical assistance, monitoring, and evaluation role and could place the local (county and municipal) agencies into a more direct, effective, integrated service delivery pattern.

MESHING OF PLANNING, SERVICE, RESEARCH, AND TRAINING

The flow of information and activity through the sequence of planning, program development, program implementation, research and development, evaluation, and training is poorly carried out at present at all levels. There is a need to orchestrate the planning, resource development, and program development activities of service and training programs, including higher education and field-based training and education programs. Furthermore, it is necessary to articulate planning and program development activities with the research, development, and dissemination programs, which are increasingly remote from the service systems, and the training programs designed to staff the service systems.

A regional policy, planning, service, training, and program development mechanism should be put in place that would provide for the unique service program responses that arise from the special local, state, and regional service needs of handicapped individuals. This regional meshing activity would bring together the necessary information, planning, service, training, and research and development programs, and would result in a more effective articulation and delivery of services than is now available.

IMPROVED MATCH OF CONSUMER-CLIENT INPUT
WITH AGENCY ORGANIZATIONAL INPUT IN
THE DEVELOPMENT AND DELIVERY OF SERVICE PROGRAMS

While consumerism has increased at a dramatic rate since the middle 1960s, the developmental disabilities act is the only major piece of federal legislation currently being implemented at the state and local level that requires consumer involvement and input into the planning, program development, and service delivery activity for handicapped individuals. The involvement of consumers, especially the handicapped, is an absolute necessity to improve the quality, timeliness, and propriety of the service needed as well as to guarantee that an appropriate and objective evaluation can be derived in the face of mounting service program costs.

A center for the development and study of consumer involvement in human services programs should be established to complement the federal, state, and regional organizations now in place.

MONITORING, EVALUATION,
AND FEEDBACK ACTIVITY IN THE PLANNING PROCESS

At the moment, information developed for planning, service, training, or research programs for handicapped individuals is not sufficiently accurate or fresh to assure the timely and effective delivery of service. Monitoring the effectiveness of programs, evaluating programs, and providing feedback to the planning and program development activity from the monitoring and evaluation activities is poorly accomplished. In addition, there is an urgent need for the development of cost-benefit studies, particularly research, into the appropriate measures of input and output of human services programs that would allow for more effective evaluation. Cost-benefit studies, thus far, have not yielded useful units of measurement or methodological approaches that would result in the program evaluation and cost-benefit statements that are available to industry and agriculture.

A special effort should be mounted to focus the issue of measurement, methodology, and systems for monitoring, evaluating, improving planning, and developing cost-benefit strategies for programs in the area of handicapped individuals.

THE MERITS OF PUBLIC EDUCATION PROGRAMS

Millions of dollars have been poured into propaganda, public awareness, and public education programs in the mental health, special education, rehabilitation, health, and other human services and human development areas. There have been differential effects, mostly measured by success in fund raising. The provision of knowledge to the general public about handicapped persons does not necessarily result in improved understanding of the nature of handicapping conditions. Neither does it always result in a positive change in the attitudes of the general public toward the handicapped and the positive contributions that the handicapped are making in our society. Furthermore, the mobilization of public interest and public support for service, training, and research and development activities in the area of the handicapped has not been as effectively accomplished as is necessary to mount the public support, attention, and resources necessary in the years ahead to prevent handicapping conditions and to provide for the special service needs of those who are and will be handicapped in our communities.

A special effort must be undertaken to study the variety of strategies that have been used effectively to mobilize public support for other issues. In addition, new approaches to public education and the strengthening of our effort to increase public awareness in the area of the handicapped must be undertaken, particularly among lower socioeconomic groups. Without a background of moral and financial support for the variety of programs needed to serve handicapped individuals, no further progress can be made and recent gains will be lost.

CLOSER COORDINATION OF GOVERNMENTAL BRANCHES

The route taken by special interest groups (notably parents) toward developing service programs for handicapped children and adults has changed. The emphasis was shifted from pressures on legislators and congressmen for specific legislation to pressures on the executive branch of state and federal government for more enlightened leadership and to a legal advocacy that maximizes utilization of the judicial branch on behalf of handicapped individuals (notably class action litigation).

There needs to be a more effective, nonpartisan coordination among the legislative, executive, and judicial branches with regard to leadership, legislative development, and legal support in order to develop a more integrated and effective network of human services programs for handicapped individuals. A mechanism should be established to assist states toward a better orchestration of legislative activity with executive agency implementation that "fits" with the judicial and legal interpretation and enforcement activities within states. In short, what we may not need is further litigation. What we do need are successful demonstrations of how current consent decrees can be fulfilled.

THE PROVISION OF ADEQUATE FINANCIAL
STABILITY DIRECTLY TO HANDICAPPED INDIVIDUALS

Social security, insurance benefits (both public and private), stipends, tax relief, job training, job provision, and other individual support strategies must be expanded and increased for handicapped persons so that an inadequate income does not hamper the handicapped person from otherwise coming to grips with the problems of community, family, and personal adjustment. A national program supported by state and local agencies and the general public must be initiated that will provide a guaranteed income through a variety of individual financial supports to handicapped persons to assure the personal welfare of each handicapped person in our society.

THE APPLICATION OF TECHNOLOGY
TO THE PROBLEMS OF HANDICAPPED PERSONS

A recent, belated effort on the part of the federal government to transfer some of the technological products developed during the active years of the space program (NASA) constitutes one of the few efforts to systematically review the current and developing technologies (hardware and software) that could be applied to alleviation of those conditions that handicap many of our citizens or to prevent the existence of those conditions that lead to handicap. The utilization of visual communications technology for diagnostic activities in rural areas, new types of materials for prosthetic devices, and computer-based instructional systems for the mentally retarded are but a few of the many opportunities that may lie in a systematic review of the full spectrum of technological development experienced in this country over the last 30 years that might be of some immediate and long-term value for handicapped persons. Similarly, those special inventions developed for handicapped persons (deaf, blind, retarded) might be of great benefit to other special populations in our country and around the world.

THE FOCUS ON DEFECT VERSUS ENVIRONMENT

The continued notion that a handicap is a defect results in persons being labeled and seen as deviant in the general society. This works against the best interests of the handicapped person and retards or perhaps precludes advances in the adequate understanding of handicapping conditions and the development of adequate service delivery systems to meet the needs of handicapped individuals.

Greater support should be given to developing and expanding the base of knowledge that has grown over the last few years, which takes an ecological approach to the understanding and alleviation of the effect of handicapping conditions, especially mental retardation. Environmental and sociocultural determinants of handicaps are poorly understood. Improved research, development, and demonstration service programs need to be mounted in order to more fully explore this major source of handicapping conditions and handicapped persons and the extent to which environmental manipulation and cultural redefinition might provide satisfactory remedial and preventive measures.

THE ROLE OF HIGHER EDUCATION

Higher education, particularly graduate schools and community colleges, is still inadequately involved in the training effort required to develop and implement a comprehensive and effective service delivery system for handicapped individuals throughout the country at the local level. The traditional role of higher education as the source of knowledge generation must change significantly in the direction of a needs-related training strategy that includes joint planning with service programs. In this way, the data base necessary to plan and develop service programs can be shared between the manpower development organizations and the service delivery systems with a consequent orchestration and synchronization between the two systems. The current situation, in which service programs are being planned and developed only to be stalled by the lack of adequate numbers and types of personnel, is unnecessary and unforgivable given the state of the art of our current planning and evaluation skills.

Higher education is, in most instances, available and willing to participate in the development of objectives, priorities, and strategies for meeting the service needs of handicapped individuals. However, an extra effort must be made to help link the institutions of higher education with the service delivery systems, especially at the state level, in order to assure adequate joint planning and program development and the successful development of competent staff, on time, for the necessary service programs. This will require special block funding to universities for correlated work with service agencies.

CONTINUING BACKUP SUPPORT SYSTEMS FOR SERVICES

Insufficient attention has been paid to the need of continuing technical assistance organizations to provide for inservice training, staff development, consultation, resource development, and the program assistance necessary to service programs on a continuing, backup support basis. Demonstration programs, information dissemination, skill development, capacity building, and technical assistance are a necessary part of any comprehensive service delivery system. Dissemination is an expensive process but one that is necessary if research products are to reach practitioners.

Technical assistance is a process whereby new knowledge, materials, special skills, and information about related service activities can be brought to even the smallest element of a comprehensive service network in a systematic way. Technical assistance organizations, typically limited to small state and regional agency staffs, must be expanded to provide the kind of continuing support and assistance necessary to help mount a significant local service delivery effort.

INADEQUATE RELATIONSHIP BETWEEN
PUBLIC EDUCATION AGENCIES AND HUMAN RESOURCES AGENCIES

Over the past several years nearly two dozen states have created "umbrella agencies," which have brought together mental health, health, rehabilitation, social services, and other human service agencies under a common bureaucratic format. In no instance is public education included in these umbrella agencies. The net effect can be to make one of the largest enterprises of value to the handicapped individual more remote from health and other human resources programs. It is important in each state to develop and maintain an adequate planning, coordination, and evaluation linkage between education and other human service programs at the state level. The situation may be particularly acute in states where state education agency heads are elected and the other state agency officials are appointed. Often this situation results in differing political backgrounds and constituencies, which can work against effective interagency program planning and program development.

This type of partisan and unnecessarily differentiated agency activity should be circumvented where possible. Cross-cutting programs, such as an Office for Children, a Department of Administration, a legislative analysis unit, or others, can be initiated in order to soften the effect of the remoteness often found between education and other state agencies around the country.

EDUCATION: THE GREATEST INVESTMENT OF RESOURCES

Despite the fact that education represents the greatest investment of resources and perhaps is of the greatest developmental benefit for the handicapped, documentation and research from the field have been relatively sparse when compared with other areas of service affecting the handicapped, such as vocational rehabilitation. However, because recent litigation and legislation are highlighting the educational needs of the handicapped, it is likely that the quantity and quality of documentation in this field will dramatically increase. This, along with a national commitment to provide full educational opportunities for all handicapped children by 1980, demands more information than currently exists. Consequently, the need for educational research, development, and dissemination (now at an all-time low ebb) is greater than ever. Personnel and funds for field-based research on practical educational problems should be developed at the federal and state level. A minimum of 15% of the service delivery system budget for education should be earmarked for research, development, and evaluation.

LACK OF SERVICES TO ELIGIBLE PERSONS

There are currently numerous federal and state programs designed to serve the handicapped that are not fully enrolled. In some cases, only about 50% of those eligible for the programs are being served. Such programs as Supplementary Security Income (SSI), Early Periodic Screening, Diagnosis and Treatment (EPSDT), and Vocational Rehabilitation programs for the severely handicapped are significantly underutilized. This is primarily due to a lack of public awareness and aggressive outreach by these programs. It is also due to the fact that the programs are not currently prepared for full enrollments in terms of finances, manpower, and organization.

Service providers must be reorganized and prepared to enroll and serve eligible persons. Services need to be promoted through public awareness campaigns. To cut costs, the red tape of screening must be reduced. When new services are developed, they should be tied as closely as possible to generic services and combined with the outreach, screening, and registration of other services directed toward the same populations.

The high cost of services, limited enrollments, service gaps, and lack of outreach result because many services addressed to the handicapped are administered out of separate agencies. For example, services like screening, food supplements, day care, early education, parent counseling, and health care for handicapped infants and toddlers are often provided by social services, public health, education, mental health, and even some private agencies. While each of these agencies may have an important role to play in the delivery of services, the duplication of administrative costs and the gaps and duplications of services must be reduced.

Counties and other local districts must develop single "ports of entry" where all service entry points converge and administrative costs are shared. This would help assure cooperation and coordination of service providers, increased public awareness, and reduce the need to search for services.

Single agencies should become responsible for the administrative costs, supervision, and coordination of services for different age levels. For example: public health from pregnancy to 5 years of age, public schools between ages 5 and 16, vocational education and rehabilitation between ages 16 and 21, social services from age 21 and up.

EXPENSIVE SERVICE DELIVERY MODELS

Many of the models of service delivery for the handicapped were developed with limited intentions and under unique service situations. Because of this, many of the service models now in use have become extremely expensive, for example, institutional care and self-contained educational classrooms. Less expensive models to deliver better quality services must be utilized, such as handicapped children in regular classrooms with resource support.

The long run cost-benefit of service models must be determined and projected so that models employed will be cost beneficial in the future, financially and socially. For example, developing 50- to 100-bed facilities to replace large institutions may be cost effective now, but over the long run may produce the same high costs of our current outmoded institutions. Solutions closer to the mainstream of life are less likely to continue to require special costs over the long run.

LACK OF ADEQUATELY TRAINED PERSONNEL

Services for the handicapped, more than ever before, require personnel who are both generalists and specialists. Service delivery personnel need to know their specialty. They also need transdisciplinary training in order to respond to the handicapped on a variety of dimensions and to know when to access other specialists. Current personnel do not often provide the full range of services needed. Too often, they access expensive, specialized services when not needed. Personnel planning services face the same dilemma; their specialized knowledge actually limits their usefulness. Manpower trained in a variety of human services areas (public health, education, and social service planning) are needed to adequately plan the coordination of comprehensive services rather than to continue the current uncoordinated, categorical, and specialized services.

Inservice training in transdisciplinary decision making for key service personnel and human service systems planners is desperately needed. Preservice and inservice training and technical assistance systems are needed to provide such continuing education for key service personnel.

HIGH OVERHEAD COSTS OF FEDERAL AND STATE PROGRAMS

Federal and state program costs have demonstrated significant increase in the last few decades. This is largely due to the confusion and mixing of planning, decision making, administering, monitoring, evaluation, reporting, and service delivery costs.

The federal and state agencies should contract for services delivered, thus retaining only the planning and monitoring costs and cutting the overhead costs of direct service delivery. Federal and state government should provide block grants to private and public agencies closer to the service level. These grants should be provided with carefully defined standards of service but with limited specifications of methods of service to be used. Federal and state governments should get out of the business of providing direct services.

NEW DIRECTIONS

It should be evident that the major need today is orchestration, consolidation, integration, and the improvement of the quality and effectiveness of the activities we now have. Therefore, a major emphasis on bold new thrusts and directions is not recommended.

Here are six innovative, new direction suggestions that should be considered:

1. There is a need for expanding and decentralizing our policy development and program evaluation processes. The development and implementation of policies and procedures related to the implementation of effective services for the handicapped has long been centralized and isolated from the main body of the service enterprise. Regional and local policy development activities need to be mounted in order to improve the quality and quantity of direct services to handicapped individuals.
2. We still work largely without a comprehensive data base of information necessary for effective planning, resource development, client tracking systems, and monitoring procedures. Without the rapid development of a comprehensive and shared information and data base, no national network of services can be effectively developed or evaluated.
3. The clear need for continuing support of service program activities begs for the establishment of regional and local technical assistance, evaluation, staff training, and management programs. Unless the service machine is continuously oiled and adjusted, it will soon become obsolete and sputter to a nonproductive halt. Technical assistance organizations, both public and private, should be continued and expanded, with the major focus directed toward the development and maintenance of effective service programs.
4. The integration of services and the coordination of planning and program activities has been recited. However, new models of coordination, collaboration, and integration of services should be developed from a basic

and applied research effort. Funds should be made available to engage organizational research and development activities to improve our attempts to maintain effective, coordinated, and integrated service systems.

5. We have yet to fully mount a comprehensive preventive services program, which would include health, economic, educational, and social services. The fundamental and long-range answer to the problem of handicapping conditions is to prevent their occurrence in the first place. Comprehensive research, development, training, and demonstration services need to be developed in the area of prevention.

6. Finally, a continuing and escalated effort must be maintained in the area of advocacy on behalf of handicapped individuals and the modification of public attitudes toward the handicapped and their place in our society. The deviancy model is still too widely held. Evaluation is still conducted toward exclusion rather than inclusion. The focus on employability and a productive slot in the corporate state still overshadows the equally important, or perhaps more important, goal of improving human development and the quality of life for the handicapped person.

REFERENCE

Gage, R.W. Integration of Human Services Delivery Systems. *Public Welfare*. Winter, 1976, 27–34.

Index